D1597741

Historic
HUDSON

Published by
Black Dome Press Corp.
1011 Route 296
Hensonville, New York 12439
www.blackdomepress.com
Tel: (518) 734-6357

First Edition Paperback 2005
Copyright © 2005 Byrne Fone
Foreword copyright © 2005 John Ashbery
Introduction copyright © 2005 Rudy Wurlitzer and Lynn Davis

Without limiting the rights under copyright above, no part of this publication may be reproduced, stored
in or introduced into a retrieval system, or transmitted, in any form, by any means (electronic, mechanical,
photocopying, recording, or otherwise), without the prior written permission of the publisher of this book.

ISBN-13: 978-1-883789-46-6
ISBN-10: 1-883789-46-X

Library of Congress Cataloging-in-Publication Data

Fone, Byrne R. S.
    Historic Hudson : an architectural portrait/Byrne Fone.—1st ed.
        p. cm.
    Includes bibliographical references and index.
    ISBN-13: 978-1-883789-46-6
    ISBN-10: 1-883789-46-X
1. Hudson (N.Y.)—Buildings, structures, etc.—Pictorial works. 2. Architecture—New York (State)—
Hudson—Pictorial works. 3. Historic buildings—New York (State)—Hudson—Pictorial works.
4.Hudson (N.Y.)—History—Pictorial works. I. Title.

    NA735.H835F65 2005
    720'.9747'39—dc22
                                2005017381

This book was made possible in part through a grant from Furthermore: a program of the J.M. Kaplan Fund.
Front cover: Batchellor's Variety store circa 1860s, Historic Hudson/Rowles Studio Collection
  of Historic Photographs.
Back cover: *View of Hudson-City and the Catskill Mountains*, engraving by W.H. Bartlett
  after William Guy Wall, circa 1837.

Design: Toelke Associates

Printed in the USA

10 9 8 7 6 5 4 3 2 1

Historic
HUDSON
An Architectural Portrait

— BYRNE FONE —

Foreword by John Ashbery

Introduction by Rudy Wurlitzer and Lynn Davis

BLACK · DOME

Dedicated
As always, to Alain.
And for historic Hudson
and Historic Hudson.

View of Hudson-City and the Catskill Mountains, *engraving by W.H. Bartlett after William Guy Wall, circa 1837.*
Collection of the author.

CONTENTS

FOREWORD

In October 1904 Henry James visited Edith Wharton at her estate, The Mount, in Lenox, Massachusetts. Back in America after a twenty-year absence, James was gathering impressions for what would become his book *The American Scene,* and not liking much of what he saw. Wharton was an indefatigable fan of the new craze for "motoring," and one day her party crossed into New York state "through zones of other manners," as James would later put it, "through images of other ideals, through densities of other values, into a separate sovereign civilization in short—this with 'a view of the autumnal Hudson' for an added incentive …" It was what today's tourists would call "leaf-peeping," though one can imagine the barely-suppressed shudder this phrase would have elicited from the Master. Alas—"Finally, the Hudson, when we reached the town that repeats in so minor a key the name of the stream, was not autumnal indeed, with majestic impenetrable mists that veiled the waters almost from sight, showing only the dim Catskills, off in space, as perfunctory graces, cheaply thrown in, and leaving us to roam the length of a large straight street which was, yes, decidedly, for comparison, for curiosity, not as the streets of Massachusetts."

After discovering for himself what all Hudson residents know—that it's hard to get a view of the river there—James and his friends "foraged for dinner—finding it indeed excellently at a quiet cook-shop, about the middle of the long-drawn way, after we had encountered coldness at the door of the main hotel by reason of our French poodle … The hospitality of the cook-shop was meanwhile touchingly, winningly unconditioned, yet full of character, of local, of national truth, as we liked to think: documentary, in a high degree—we talked it over—for American life … It was the queer old complexion of the long straight street, however, that most came home to me: Hudson, in the afternoon quiet, seemed to stretch back, with fumbling friendly hand, to the earliest outlook of my consciousness. Many matters had come and gone, innumerable impressions had supervened; yet here, in the stir of the senses, a whole range of small forgotten things revived, things intensely Hudsonian, more than Hudsonian; small echoes and tones and sleeping lights, small sights and sounds and smells that made one, for an hour, as small—carried one up the rest of the river, the very river of life, indeed, as a thrilled, roundabouted pilgrim, by primitive steamboat, to a mellow, medieval Albany."

It's not quite clear whether James is alluding to childhood memories—his father was born and raised in Albany—or whether he and Wharton actually proceeded upriver by "primitive steamboat"—their car had stopped in Hudson for repairs, and might conceivably have been out of commission. It's also unclear what he means by "things intensely Hudsonian." Presumably he was alluding to the river, though he could have

Historic Hudson ❁ An Architectural Portrait

passed through the town long before. What is clear is that the place touched a rare (for rural America) sympathetic chord in him. The "long straight street" is forgiven for its straightness—so unlike the distinguished winding streets of Massachusetts and of Europe—and the town welcomes him "with fumbling friendly hand." He couldn't know that Hudson's official nickname would one day be "The Friendly City." Yet something in the very plainness of the place spoke to him. James wasn't often an advocate of plainness, but he was seldom deceived by "fancy" manners either. Hudson's uncompromising grid of streets (it was, Byrne Fone tells us, the first planned city in America), offset by its appealing jumble of architectural styles, became just for a moment what James had earlier termed "The Great Good Place."

The city's architecture has suffered over the years, sometimes from fire and other accidental causes, more often from neglect, sometimes from instinctive hostility toward what is old and distinguished—think of William Carlos Williams' line "Beat hell out of it/Beautiful Thing." That animosity may have caused the destruction of the by-all-accounts lovely General Worth Hotel (perhaps the very one where James was turned away) during the sixties "urban renewal" craze—a misnomer if ever there was one. In any case the hotel was summarily leveled and replaced by not much of anything. Today there is new awareness of just how valuable, both aesthetically and monetarily, our architectural heritage is. As many of Hudson's old buildings undergo or await restoration, this book's long-overdue visual record of its treasures should provide a further inducement toward preserving what has so miraculously been handed down to us—nothing less than "a whole range of small forgotten things …, things intensely Hudsonian, more than Hudsonian."

John Ashbery
Hudson, 5/24–5/31/2005

Henry James quotes are from pp. 50–52 of *The American Scene* (New York: Scribners, 1946).

John Ashbery is the author of more than twenty books of poetry and has won many major American awards for his work including the Pulitzer Prize for Poetry, the National Book Critics Circle Award, the National Book Award, the Bollingen Prize, and the Frank O'Hara Prize. He is the first English-language poet to win the Grand Prix de Biennales Internationales de Poésie. He has received fellowships from the Academy of American Poets, the Fulbright Foundation, the Guggenheim Foundation, and the MacArthur Foundation, and is a former Chancellor of the Academy of American Poets. John Ashbery is currently the Charles P. Stevenson, Jr., Professor of Languages and Literature at Bard College.

INTRODUCTION

In the spring of 1991, we turned off the Taconic Parkway and made a detour through the city of Hudson. As we drove up the length of Warren Street—the city's main thoroughfare—we experienced an eerie sensation, as if we had slipped through a scrim of time and landed at the tail end of the nineteenth century.

On both sides of the street stood rows of largely untouched Federal, Greek Revival, Victorian, and Queen Anne structures, as well as a few jarring examples of urban renewal from the 1960s including a soulless low-income high-rise reminiscent of South Bronx urban blight. As we continued towards the center of town, we passed abandoned storefronts and bars boarded up with plywood. There were only a few cars, and the sidewalks were deserted except for what looked like a huddle of crack dealers lurking in front of a pizza joint. Everywhere there were examples of decay and urban paralysis. It seemed to be a suspended realm removed from progress or hope, a place—in the words of Edgar Allen Poe—where "All that we see or seem, is but a dream within a dream."

Such was our introduction to Hudson, a dying city composed of a shrinking population of less than 8,000 people, its once prosperous streets formally laid out on a nine-block grid running west to east from the Hudson River.

A few months later, seeking an interlude from the distractions and density of Manhattan, we remembered Hudson. We rented and then finally bought an 1835 Federal house across the street from the post office. The house had formerly belonged to the Presbyterian Church, and in the late 1880s a wing had been added in the Italianate style by A. J. Davis. Directly across a small park, surrounded on two sides by Victorian townhouses, we could see the courthouse that had been built by the firm of Warren and Wetmore, which later built Grand Central Station. That winter Lynn photographed every building on Warren Street—an archival homage to the city that has since been donated to Historic Hudson, the city's volunteer historic preservation organization.

The community we found ourselves in was not without problems. Hudson has always been a boom-and-bust town. Its architectural integrity has survived toxic coal-fired cement plants, nondescript malls on its borders, corrupt cops and city officials, as well as elements that gave the city a frontier reputation for anarchy and lawlessness—drug dealers, petty criminals, prostitutes, and gamblers.

In the decade or more that we have lived in Hudson, we have seen an influx of people who favor an environmental economy that would—among other benefits—protect the city's architectural heritage. These newcomers were often at odds with some of the older residents who felt a lingering nostalgia for the days when various forms of industry dominated the town.

At the turn of the twenty-first century, Hudson seems to have awakened from one of its periodic slumbers, but the city's fragile existence faces new dangers. Hudson's architecture has become vulnerable to new threats from gentrification and land speculators armed with plans for condominium sprawl and gated communities. It is a time of accelerated change in the post-9/11 Hudson River Valley, and especially in the city of Hudson itself, as families and small-business entrepreneurs flee the increasing claustrophobia and financial stress of New York City.

Given that impermanence is inevitable, one can be grateful that the shifting population of Hudson, with all the attendant tensions and confrontations of a cultural collision, is evidence that the city is surviving and involved in the ongoing drama of reinventing itself, again.

Historic Hudson: An Architectural Portrait, with its incomparable trove of photographs from the nineteenth and early twentieth centuries, depicts what Hudson was and illustrates why it was and is so much admired by so many visitors and residents, both old and new. These remarkable images capture both the elegance and the grittiness of the city, provide a detailed and unique record of its public and domestic architecture, recall the reality of its vanished industry, and act as sometimes painful reminders of the elegance of our lost heritage.

When Lynn photographed Warren Street—she called the series the *Warren Street Project*—we were pleased and inspired to find that so much of the architectural fabric of early Hudson remained intact. *Historic Hudson: An Architectural Portrait* confirms this survival. The history of the city of Hudson that Byrne Fone offers—the first to my knowledge that surveys the story of Hudson from its beginning to the present day—frames the photographs with a scholarly, yet eloquent commentary, and provides a lively and readable guide along that long and winding road from the eighteenth to the twenty-first century.

Rudy Wurlitzer
Lynn Davis
Hudson, New York
May, 2005

Rudy Wurlitzer has written five novels—*Nog, Flats, Quake, Slow Fade,* and *The Drop Edge of Yonder*—as well as two nonfiction books, *Travel to Sacred Places* and *Walker.* He has also written two plays, an opera composed by Philip Glass based on Kafka's *In the Penal Colony,* and over a dozen produced screenplays including Sam Peckinpah's *Pat Garrett and Billy the Kid, Two Lane Blacktop, Walker,* Volker Schlondorff's *Voyager,* Bernardo Bertolucci's *Little Buddha,* and *Candy Mountain,* which he codirected with Robert Frank.

Lynn Davis has had over fifty solo exhibitions. Her work has been exhibited internationally and her photographs are in public and private collections around the world, including the Museum of Modern Art, the J. Paul Getty Museum, the Chicago Museum of Contemporary Art, Harvard University, and the Houston Museum of Fine Arts. Selections of her African images appeared in *Wonders of the African World* by Henry Louis Gates. This was followed by her second monograph, *Monument,* and her third, *American Monument.* Davis is represented by the Edwynn Houk Gallery in New York City.

PREFACE

LOOKING AT HUDSON

Hudson's past is preserved pictorially far better than that of many other small towns in America. The landscape and the river views around the city were among the favorite subjects of the Hudson River School of American painters that included Thomas Cole, Sanford Robinson Gifford (a Hudson native), Henry Ary, Arthur Parton, and Frederic Church—who built his Moorish mansion, Olana, in the highlands above Hudson. Many of these artists recorded on canvas their impressions of Hudson and the Hudson River well into the late nineteenth century.

Hudson's past also is preserved in a unique photographic collection. From the 1860s to the mid-twentieth century, Hudson was photographically depicted first by Frank Forshew (a local Hudson professional photographer) and from the beginning of the twentieth century to the 1930s by Forshew's successor, Samuel Rowles. This collection records a century of images of the city—public events, people, streets, houses, and public buildings. Many of the buildings captured on film by Forshew and Rowles have now disappeared and are remembered and documented only in these photographs. Many more structures are still sound and in use, but are different in appearance than they were. Few towns of any size possess such a unique collection of images that so comprehensively opens windows into the past. They show us the story of this city, confirm its history, and reveal vanished fragments of the past.

They also bear witness to the unfortunate consequences that can result when our heritage is thought to be of little value. In these images from the past, published herein for the first time to celebrate the 220th anniversary of Hudson's incorporation, can be seen not only the history of one small town, but the changing face of small-town America.

WRITING HUDSON

The story of Hudson has been told in some detail by several writers—mostly Hudson residents—whose passion for (if not always their approval of) the progress of the city is evident in their texts. The earliest long account is by A. Gorham Worth, writing under the name of Ignatius Jones. His *Recollections of Hudson* (1847) is a fond, if somewhat tart and doleful, reminiscence by one who was there near the beginning of the city's rise and who upon revisiting in 1847 declared Hudson a "dead town." Worth's gloomy assessment was not without basis, but it is no doubt overdrawn. As Ruth Piwonka once wrote, *Recollections of Hudson* is more "a lament for and not a history of times passed."

Stephen B. Miller followed with his *Sketches of Hudson* in 1862. Miller was as enthusiastic as Worth was dubious, carefully detailing Hudson's early history, providing the fullest account then available of the city's rise, and forecasting a cheerful estimate of its future. A few years later, in 1878, Captain Franklin Ellis drew heavily upon Miller for Hudson's early history when he wrote *History of Columbia County,* but Ellis added a wealth of detail about the founding of Hudson's schools, churches, and industries, and also provided complete lists of Hudson's mayors and other officials starting from the incorporation of the city in 1785. Anna Bradbury, using both Miller and Ellis, wrote her *History of the City of Hudson, N.Y.* in 1908. Bradbury's book is a charming and very useful insider history. She clearly knew everyone and had opinions about everything, which she does not hesitate to make known.

Several useful twentieth-century texts have looked at the city's past. Mary R. Wend's "The Administrative Effects of the Breakdown of Law Enforcement in Hudson, New York" (1962), an unpublished thesis for New York University's Graduate School of Public Administration, provides important insights into mid-twentieth-century Hudson. Chapters on Hudson appear in Ruth Piwonka and Roderic H. Blackburn's book *A Visible Heritage: Columbia County, New York; A History in Art and Architecture* (1977) and in Ruth Piwonka's exhibition catalog *Mount Merino, Views of Mount Merino, South Bay, and the City of Hudson Painted by Henry Ary and His Contemporaries* (1978). Piwonka also discussed the early days of the city in "Hudson," an article in *Hudson Valley Regional Review* (1985). Bruce Hall, in *Diamond Street: The Story of the Little Town with the Big Red Light District* (1994), provided an entertaining look at the city's underside.

More recently, in *Hudson's Merchants and Whalers: The Rise and Fall of a River Port, 1783–1850* (2004), Margaret Schram presented a careful, detailed, and definitive discussion of Hudson's whaling past, replacing myth with history.

ACKNOWLEDGMENTS

In preparing this book I have been fortunate enough to have benefited from the encouragement and advice of many people who love Hudson and its history, and who have shared their time, knowledge, and materials that they possess or to which they have access. Two people merit special recognition.

Carole Osterink has been especially generous in sharing her extensive, informed, sensitive, and precise knowledge of the city's history and of its architectural and cultural geography. She has read the manuscript with a careful eye and offered valuable suggestions for its revision. As president of Historic Hudson—the city's all-volunteer, not-for-profit preservation and historical society—Carole gave approval for the use in this book of the extensive collection of nineteenth and early-twentieth-century photographs of the city taken by Frank Forshew and Samuel Rowles, known as the Historic Hudson/Rowles Studio Collection of Historic Photographs. Unless otherwise indicated, all of the photographic images in this book are taken from this collection.

Jeremiah Rusconi is a longtime Hudson resident and one of the very first to recognize precisely why Hudson is often called "a dictionary of American architecture." His nearly unrivaled knowledge of the historical context and the architectural history of the city, as well as his encyclopedic professional knowledge of the specific material details of Hudson's architecture—almost building by building—make him an unparalleled source of information. His personal collection of Hudsoniana, including artifacts and images, is a remarkable and unique resource. To Jeremiah and the late David Whitcomb, the city and Historic Hudson owe a debt of gratitude for the survival of the glass-plate negatives that make up the Historic Hudson/Rowles Studio Collection.

For additional images of Hudson, I am indebted to the following: the late Hank DiCintio, who together with Debbie DiCintio generously allowed me the use of their extensive collection; Harry B. Halaco, who allowed me access to his collection of early-twentieth-century postcard views of Hudson; and Sedat Pakay, photographer and documentary filmmaker, who photographed especially for this book several images of Hudson today.

A grateful nod of thanks must go to Margaret B. Schram, incomparable chronicler of the city, who read the manuscript and made many valuable suggestions.

I wish to recognize and thank the Hudson Area Association Library and the Columbia County Historical Society for allowing me access and permission to reproduce materials in their collections.

Deborah Allen, the owner and publisher of Black Dome Press, has been an unending source of support and encouragement; Steve Hoare has elegantly edited the text.

Further contributions to the text were made by proofreaders Matina Billias, Natalie Mortensen, Erin Mulligan, Eric Raetz, and Ed Volmar. A diligent job of indexing was performed by Bob Gildersleeve.

Toelke Associates did a superb and beautiful job designing the book so that it perfectly complements the text and images.

I wish to thank the Ettinger Foundation for a very generous grant in support of the long-term preservation and conservation of the original negatives of the Historic Hudson/Rowles Studio Collection.

This book could not have been produced without a very generous grant from Furthermore: a program of the J.M. Kaplan Fund, which provided crucial underwriting support for several aspects of the book, most especially the reproduction of all of the Historic Hudson/ Rowles Studio Collection glass-plate negatives.

I want to thank Sedat Pakay for carefully and sensitively reproducing from the Historic Hudson/Rowles Studio Collection's glass-plate negatives the lion's share of the images that appear in this book.

My very special thanks and affection go to Lynn Davis and Rudy Wurlitzer, true Hudsonians, who kindly read the book in manuscript and wrote a lovely and personal foreword to it in which they tell us just how Hudson first caught their perceptive eyes.

I am equally grateful to and especially pleased to thank John Ashbery for so beautifully reminding us, in his meditation on Henry James' visit to Hudson, that for those with perceptive eyes, Hudson has always had sights and sounds that stir the senses and bemuse.

I am always grateful to Alain Pioton, whose support was as unwavering as it was invaluable, even as he lived through the throes of creation.

Frank Forshew (1827–1895) specialized in portrait photography and was one of the most well-known photographers of the late nineteenth century. His photographs of the city of Hudson, and those taken by his successor at Rowles Studio, comprise the bulk of the images in this book.

PROLOGUE

HUDSON: A DICTIONARY OF AMERICAN ARCHITECTURE

No one who has visited Hudson can be unaware of the historic and architectural treasures possessed by this small upstate city on the banks of the Hudson River. To walk its streets is to see nearly every residential architectural style invented or adapted in America. Eighteenth and nineteenth-century residences stand nearer the river, while mid and late-nineteenth-century houses and mansions line the middle blocks. Compact and comfortable houses from the 1920s and 1930s are found in the upper reaches. To visit the seven-block-long commercial heart of the city on Warren Street as it marches up from the river to the Hudson city park is to view a panorama of three centuries of American architecture in one, mile-long stretch.

Nantucket-style saltboxes, Federal, Greek Revival, Gothic Revival, mid-century Victorian, towered and turreted late Victorian, Italianate, stick-style houses of the 1880s, Second Empire, Queen Anne and Colonial Revival homes of the 1890s, Romanesque, Academic revival, Arts and Crafts bungalows of the 1920s and 1930s, as well as less grand, early-twentieth-century "comfortable homes" of shingle, stucco, and brick—all are represented in Hudson. Though rightly admired for its eighteenth-century houses (both large and modest) or praised for its mid-century mansions, an equally important part of Hudson's treasury is the large number of relatively intact mid and late-nineteenth-century, middle-class houses that add a remarkable variety and diversity to the mix of earlier styles. It is because of this that Hudson has been called, by one modern architectural historian, "a dictionary of American architectural design." Hudson's visible heritage, a fabric that so many small towns have lost or deliberately destroyed, is indeed an invaluable lesson in the history of American architecture.

When we look back at Hudson's history—its founding and rise to economic eminence in the eighteenth century, its economic ups and downs in the nineteenth century, its descent into economic somnolence in the early and mid-twentieth century, followed by its recent renaissance in the late twentieth century and early twenty-first century—we can trace the economic life of the nation in microcosm. When we look at the collection of paintings and photographs that so extensively details Hudson's long architectural history, many of them showing scenes and houses that have now disappeared forever, we can see there, in brief, the iconography of the nation.

Hudson's early architectural boom began when it was a thriving and prosperous city in the late eighteenth and early nineteenth century. To house its newfound wealth, Hudson constructed along its main street a row of elegant commercial buildings, most of which are still intact today. To house the owners of this wealth, grand mansions were built in the elegant Federal and Greek Revival styles. From the city's founding in 1783 and its incorporation as a city in 1785 until well near the end of the nineteenth century (despite the effects of periodic economic misfortunes and two devastating fires that destroyed much of southwestern Hudson), residents continued to erect imposing commercial structures and elegant family homes, building farther and farther uptown away from the riverfront.

The founding and building of Hudson was a grand and imaginative experiment undertaken by a group of New England merchants calling themselves the Proprietors. These entrepreneurs came up the Hudson River in 1783 to find a safe harbor where they could rebuild the trading empire that they had lost by the end of the Revolutionary War. They found the tiny frontier hamlet of Claverack Landing on the banks of the Hudson. It seemed just right, so they bought it all. Though their intention and vision were practical—to establish a safe harbor for trade—to do so they had to engage in a breathtaking and courageous undertaking. They proposed to do nothing less than to build, virtually out of nothing, a modern city. Thanks to the energy and vision of these founding fathers, Hudson grew in just a few years from a small settlement with two waterfront docks with a handful of inhabitants to a bustling town that could claim to be the first city to be chartered under the flag of the new United States of America (in 1785) and the first city in the new nation to be built as a planned community.

When building began in earnest in the late eighteenth century, the Proprietors were satisfied only with the best. Materials and workmanship of the highest quality went into the construction, and the structures they built, many of which stand today, were exemplars of the latest in architectural theory and design. Indeed, it might be argued that eighteenth-century Hudson was a laboratory for architectural experiment. By the end of 1786, Hudson was known not only as a busy engine of trade, but as a city that was setting a distinguished example of the best in contemporary American architecture.

When the Proprietors first arrived from New England, a few of them may have carried with them the frames of simple, New England-style houses. They were also familiar, of course, with the eighteenth-century American version of Georgian architecture and the Federal style that followed it; houses in both styles were built in Hudson. The new, Greek revival style began to appear in the early nineteenth century.

Greek Revival replaced Federal as the favored style by the 1820s and 1830s. Many Federal houses in Hudson were modernized in the Greek Revival style in the 1830s. This influence can be seen in many of Hudson's houses and commercial buildings, and the style remained fashionable until about 1860.

As the city grew, not only did its residents venture into the construction of every conceivable style of fashionable architecture, they also experimented in many kinds of economic endeavor. By the end of the eighteenth century, Hudson's port was second only to New York City's in terms of volume of trade in New York State. Entrepreneurs, merchants, shipbuilders, and whalers home from the sea walked Hudson's streets. Shipbuilding yards, sailmaking, rope, oil and candle works, factories for processing the materials derived from whaling, tanneries, and small wool mills fueled Hudson's economy.

This prosperity was interrupted by the economic downturn that followed the War of 1812 and led to nearly two decades of decline. The shipbuilding and whaling industries languished. Then, in the 1830s, Hudsonians turned back to these bulwarks of economic vitality, and Hudson's whaling fleet and trading vessels sailed again. The revival was brief. By mid-century, Hudson's early sea trade–based economy failed, this time for good. The legend of Hudson as primarily a whaling town, and even as *the* whaling town in America is, in fact, the product of nostalgia and romance rather than reality. Whaling was an important industry for Hudson, but it was the varied merchant trade conducted by its port that gave the city the wherewithal to build its mansions.

By mid-century, Hudson had turned from harvesting the fruits of the sea to processing the products of the earth. It seemed as if the good times had returned. Hudson had become a destination for the railroad, one line of which had been built across the South Bay to carry ore to the new ironworks built on pilings and landfill in the bay. For a few years Hudson made stoves and other iron products, and mills produced a variety of goods. Breweries opened, as did a tobacco factory. Progress and industry were the catchwords of the day.

This return of wealth at mid-century spurred new construction. From the 1850s to the end of the nineteenth century, many new buildings were constructed in the styles known as Victorian. Gothic Revival was followed by the Italianate style. This gave way to the heavier Second Empire style. Then a number of revival styles appeared—Queen Anne, Romanesque, and stick-style houses that were simpler forms of the Gothic. At the end of the 1800s and during the beginning of the 1900s, Hudson houses were built in all the latest architectural fashions—Colonial Revival, Classical, Academic Revival, and American Arts and Crafts.

In Hudson, as elsewhere in the nation, economic cycle followed cycle: the heady days of the eighteenth century, the slow decline of the early nineteenth century, the revival at mid-century, the panic of the 1870s, the revival of the 1880s, and the long depression of 1893. By the end of the nineteenth century, Hudson was no longer an important river port or a hub of industry. The great days of Hudson's prosperity were over, and so too were the great days of its architectural achievement. Save for the construction of one or two new buildings in the city in the early twentieth century—the most notable being the important county courthouse—nothing new of note was built.

In the early twentieth century, many residents hoped that the glory days of economic prominence might return with the opening of the Portland Cement Company, which mined limestone from the hills above Hudson and processed it on the site of the defunct Hudson Iron Works, where the South Bay once existed. For a time it seemed as if that wish might come true. Cement became Hudson's largest industry for the next half century. Nearly 1,200 people worked in the two cement plants then operating, and others found work in the knitting mills that had opened in the city in the 1890s. Hudson's main street thrived again. But it could not, and did not, last. The Great Depression came, signaling the end.

The post–Depression recovery era and the war years brought some relief, but the closing of the two cement plants in the late 1970s put an end to that. Hudson was once again, as an early-nineteenth-century Jeremiah had called it, a "finished city."

Either because no one could afford to or was interested in saving them, many of Hudson's mansions and elegantly simple buildings rode through time unappreciated and neglected. Some were abandoned, and some were demolished.

In the early 1980s, however, Hudson once again began to renew itself as it had in the late eighteenth and mid-nineteenth centuries. Hudson's long history demonstrates how it was periodically renewed and enriched by the arrival of new people with new ideas and different ways of life, beginning with the arrival of the Proprietors in 1783. A new wave of settlers in the 1980s continued that long tradition of rebirth and revitalization. By the end of the twentieth century, the architecture and unique character of the city of Hudson came to be avidly appreciated once again. Many of its houses have been saved and restored by new devotees—the spiritual, if not the actual, heirs of those first Proprietors who found a sleepy boat landing and turned it into something grand.

Hudson's newest settlers have undeniably changed the city. They saw a cityscape ready to be recreated and set to work doing so with enthusiasm. The seeds of a renewed city were planted and changes were begun. The last twenty years have witnessed rich rewards and continued high enthusiasm.

Enthusiasm is not enough, however. The heritage of Hudson is precious; its architecture is important, and its past is rich and complex. The façades of the buildings lining Hudson's streets tell the story of the city's past. Hudson's buildings also constitute the built environment in which the affairs of daily lives are conducted in the present. Most importantly, they are the assets of Hudson's future, and hence irreplaceable and invaluable.

Those fortunate enough to own one or more of Hudson's buildings are thus not only proprietors of the city's past, but of its present and future, and with ownership goes stewardship. Stewardship means that today's owners (only temporary proprietors after all) hold their properties in trust for the future. As stewards they must maintain, improve, preserve, and eventually hand over these buildings as intact as possible. As good stewards they have an obligation to pass on to future generations a better, not diminished, city that respects the integrity of the history and architectural style of individual buildings and the larger architectural and neighborhood context in which they stand.

No one advocates preservation for the sake of making the city of Hudson yet another museum village. But when a historic building—whether great or small, grand or simple, public or private—is lost through demolition, altered beyond recognition on a personal whim or through ill-advised or hurried remodeling without thought to its style or history, or "revived" as something it never was, then not only is a document of the city's history lost, but yet another defeat is suffered in the effort to keep alive the vital record of the past that is the most important blueprint for comprehending the present.

Over time, the various economic ventures that shaped Hudson have disappeared: its mercantile trade is long gone; its whaling industry is a nostalgic memory; its busy shipyards can barely be traced on the river's edge; its wool mills are empty shells; its various factories lie derelict or demolished. The economies that created them have vanished, but Hudson's buildings have survived. It may be that the economies that fuel the current renaissance will one day vanish as well. But despite the many depredations to Hudson's physical appearance caused over time by decay, neglect, and failed economies, the city of Hudson has retained the lion's share of its architectural heritage and thus a wealth of invaluable material evidence of its social and architectural history. That this is so is surely a cause for celebration, even as the survival of this heritage must also be a constant reminder of the ever-present need for continuing vigilance in its protection and preservation.

Viewing the city of Hudson from Mt. Merino in the early twentieth century.

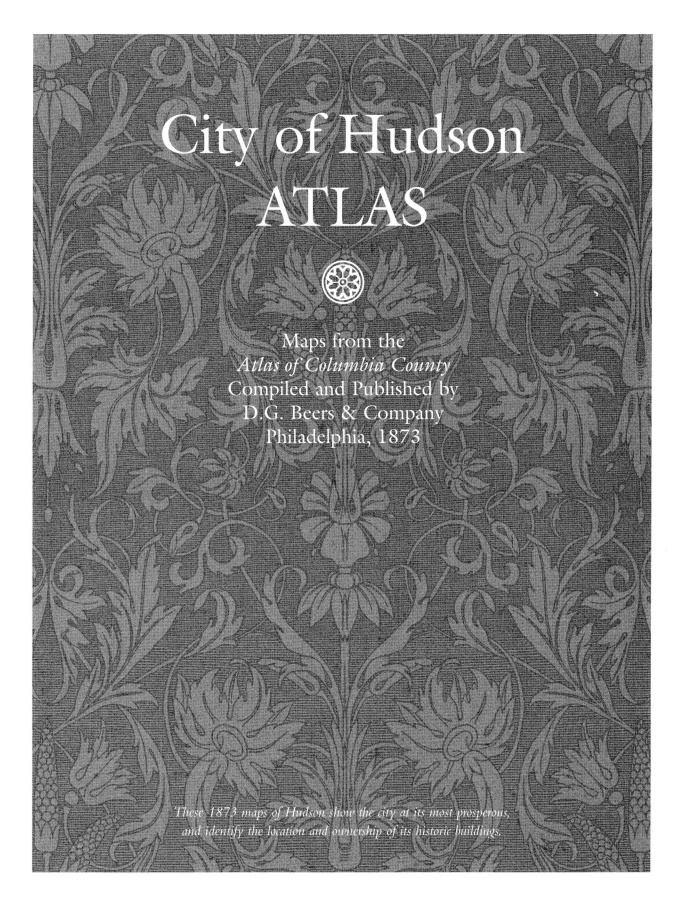

City of Hudson ATLAS

Maps from the
Atlas of Columbia County
Compiled and Published by
D.G. Beers & Company
Philadelphia, 1873

*These 1873 maps of Hudson show the city at its most prosperous,
and identify the location and ownership of its historic buildings.*

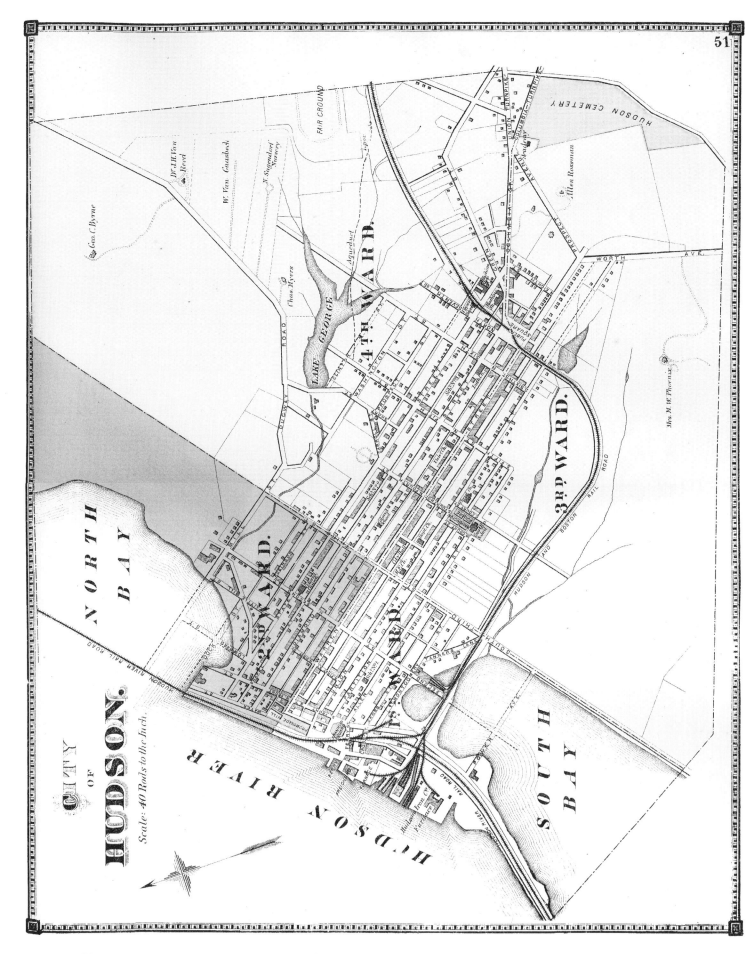

Historic Hudson ✦ An Architectural Portrait

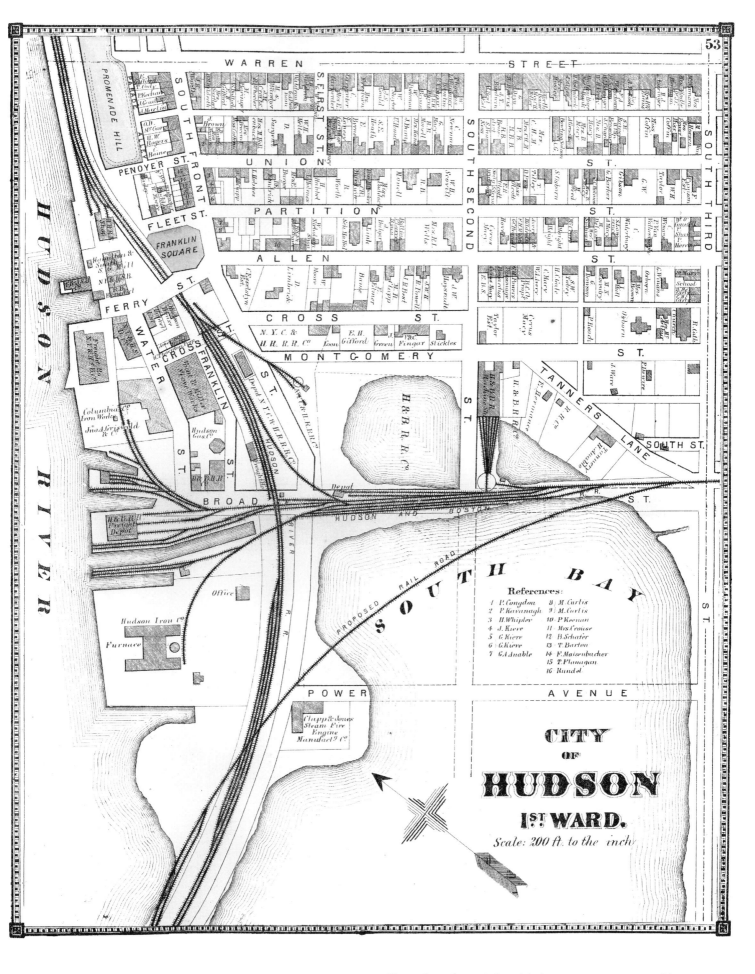

References:
1 P. Congdon   8 M. Curtis
2 P. Kavanagh   9 M. Curtis
3 H. Whipler   10 P. Keenan
4 J. Kiere   11 Mrs. Crouse
5 G. Kiere   12 B. Schafer
6 G. Kiere   13 T. Barton
7 G.A. Anable   14 F. Maisenbacker
                              15 T. Flanigan
                              16 Rundel

CITY OF HUDSON
1ST WARD.

Scale: 200 ft. to the inch

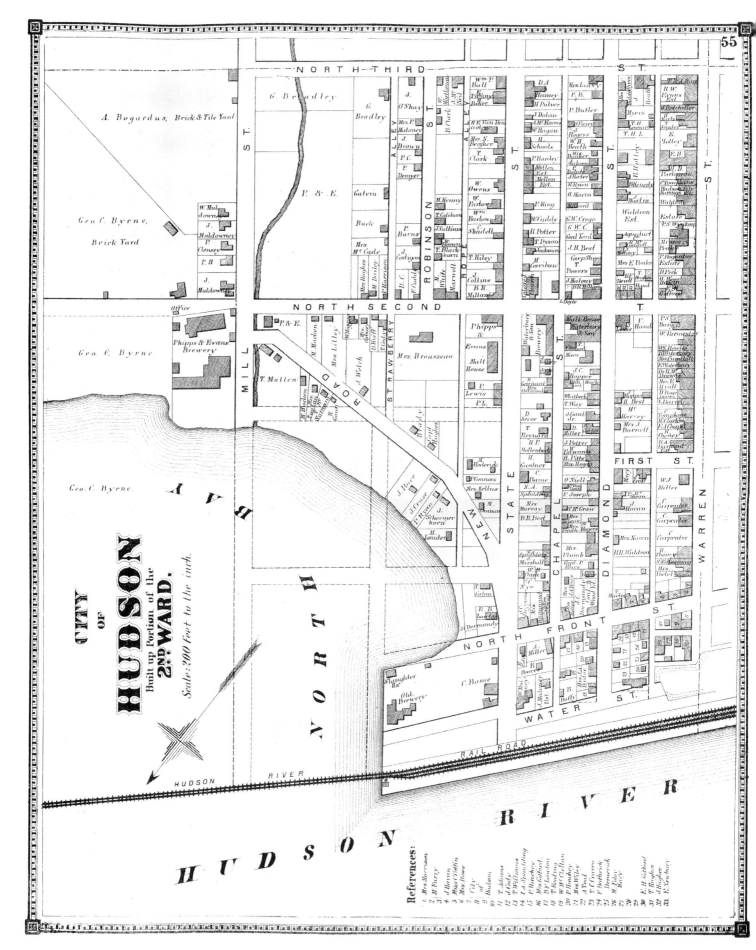

CITY OF HUDSON

Built up Portion of the

2ND WARD.

Scale: 200 feet to the inch.

References:

1. Mrs. Harrison
2. M. Perry
3. J. Herron
4. J. Herron
5. Bast Cinfin
6. Mrs. Bowe
7. City
8. of
9. Hudson
10. T. Adams
11. J. Fody
12. T. Williams
13. L. A. Spaulding
14. P. Hockey
15. Mrs. Gibbols
16. B. F. Lawton
17. B. Kenney
18. W. McClellan
19. P. Hushey
20. Mrs. Wiley
21. A. Teal
22. T. Craven
23. F. Bethrick
24. F. Denerick
25. M. Edey
26. M. Macy
27. E. H. Gifford
28. T. Hughes
29. E. Newbury

Historic Hudson ◉ An Architectural Portrait

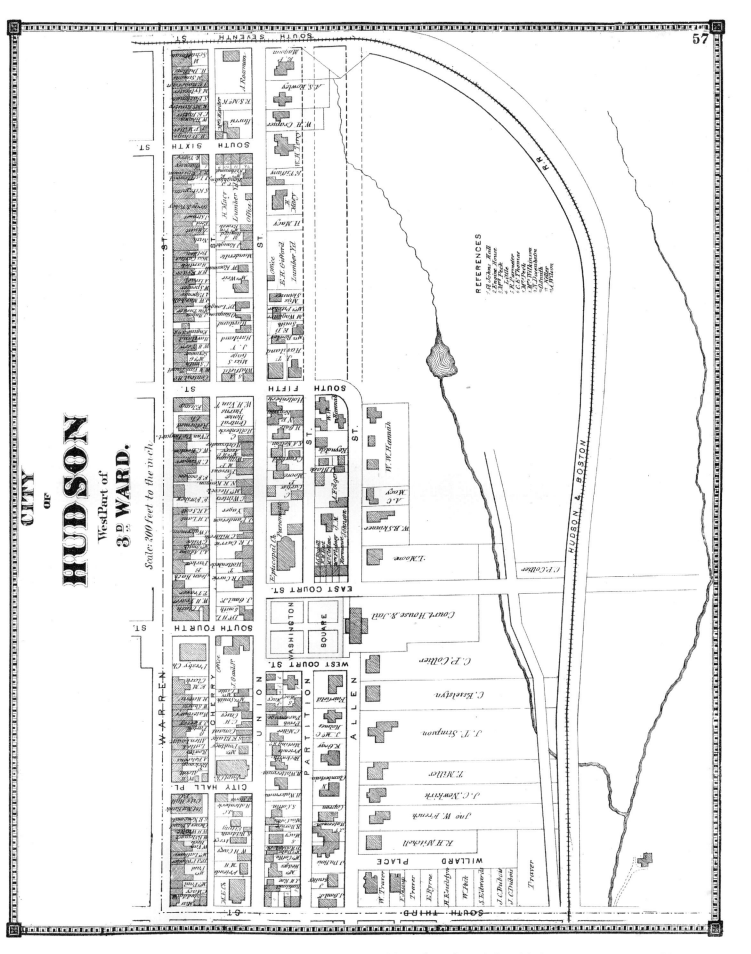

City of Hudson Atlas, 1873

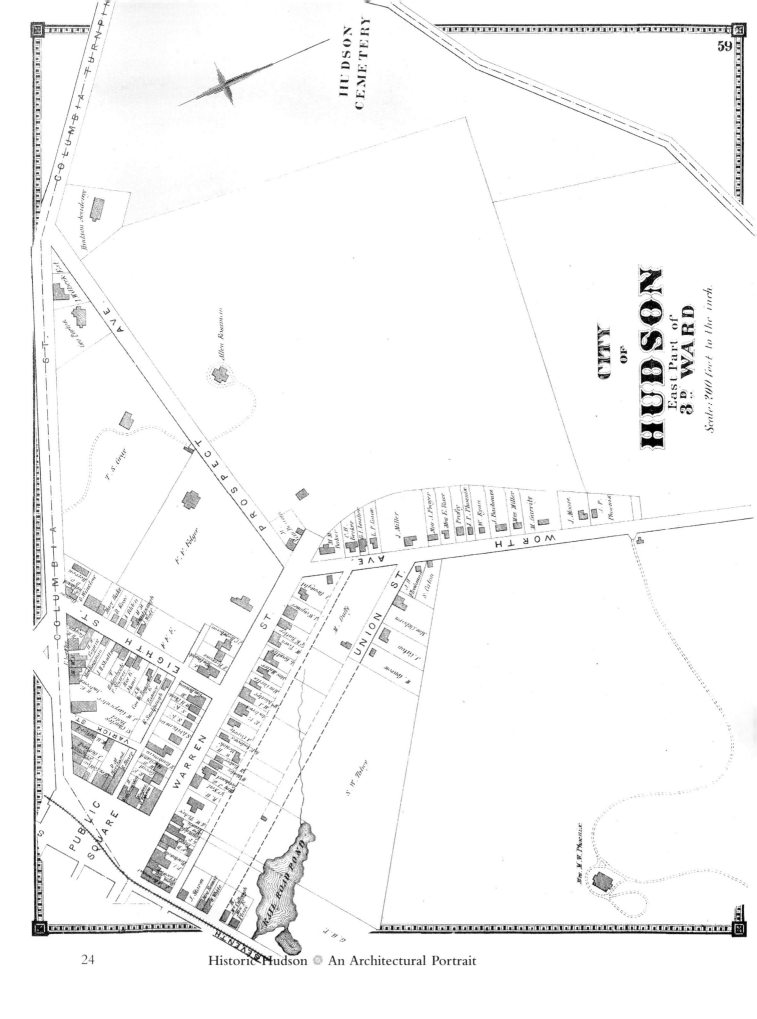

CITY OF

HUDSON

East Part of

3ᴰ WARD

Scale: 200 feet to the inch.

HUDSON CEMETERY

COLUMBIA TURNPIKE

PROSPECT AVE

COLUMBIA ST.

WORTH AVE

UNION ST.

EIGHTH ST.

VARICK ST.

WARREN ST.

PUBLIC SQUARE

SEVENTH

KITE ROW POND

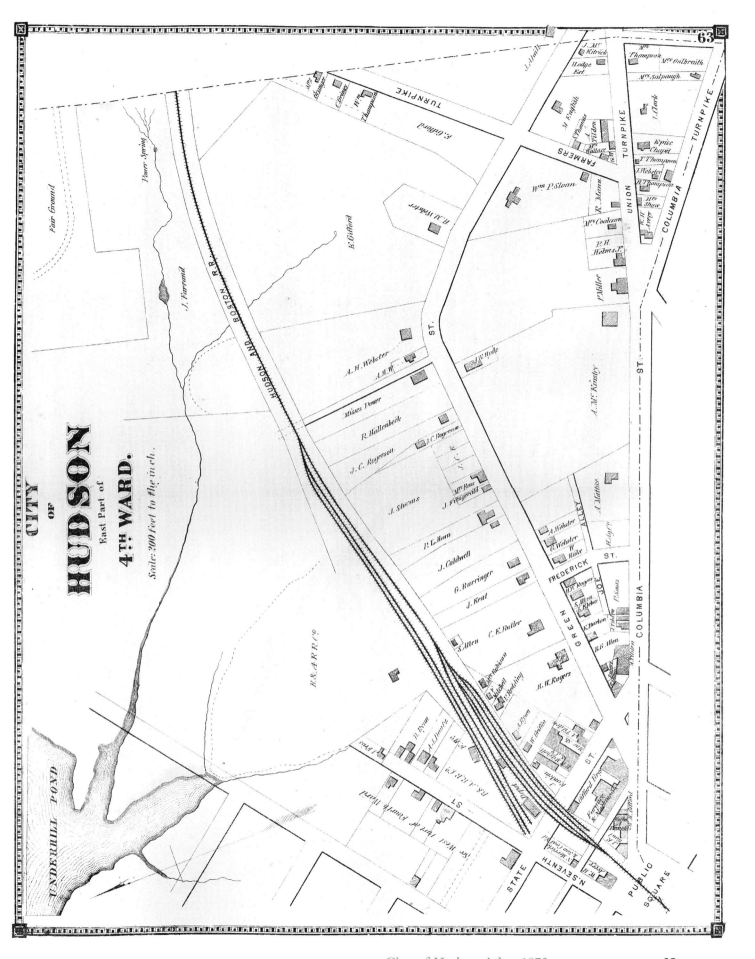

CITY OF HUDSON
East Part of
4TH WARD.
Scale 200 Feet to the inch.

63

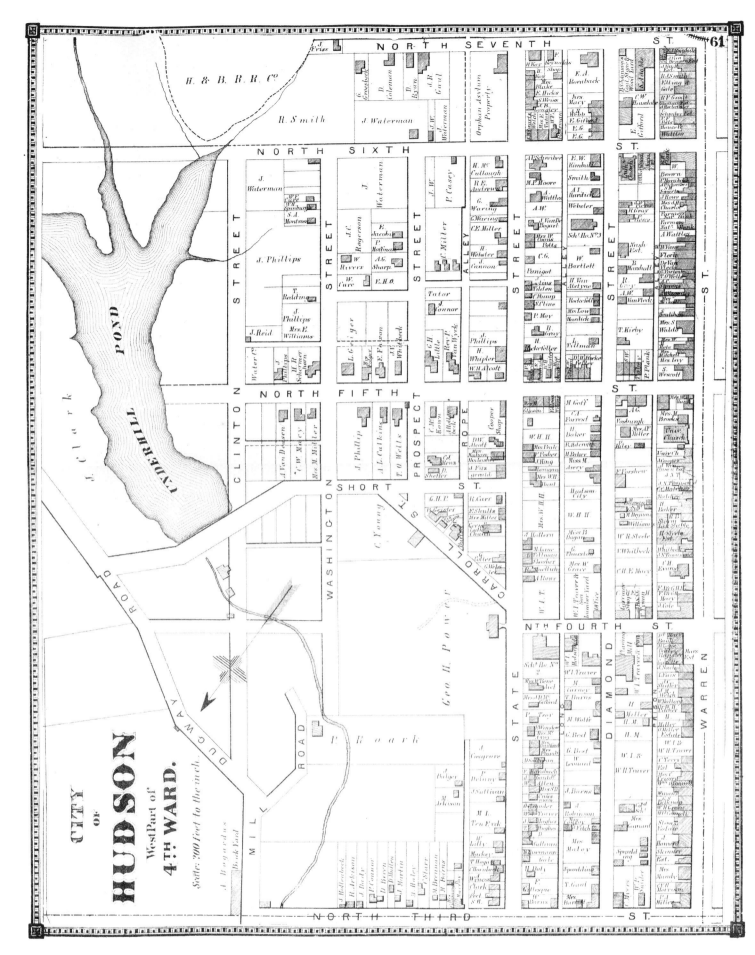

ONE

MAY 3, 1785

The ships in the harbor at the river's edge displayed their colors from every mast, flags were raised from every eminence, and thirteen cannon were fired in celebration on May 3, 1785, when Ezekiel Gilbert, Esq., having come up the Hudson River from New York City, delivered the charter for the new city of Hudson. To the rejoicing crowds—who according to an eyewitness engaged in "every possible demonstration of gratification"—the newly appointed mayor, Seth Jenkins, issued a proclamation declaring that the settlement of Hudson had been raised to the dignity of a city, its act of incorporation having been approved by the General Assembly of New York State on April 22, 1785. The citizens were justly proud, for though Hudson was not the first community in the state to be made a city (it was, in fact, the third), it could claim a special and unique distinction—it was the first city to be chartered after the Declaration of Independence. Thus, it was the first chartered city in the United States.

But there were more reasons than that for celebration. The riverfront boasted a large new wharf and two shipbuilding yards. Everywhere, houses and stores were being constructed on the newly laid out streets. Hudson was prosperous and its citizens were wealthy. Indeed, some felt, as the author of *Men and Times of the Revolution* wrote, "In 1788, I visited the new city of Hudson which exhibited a progress at that time almost without parallel in American history."[1]

The People of the Waters That Are Never Still

Just a very few years before, none of this existed. Not only was Hudson not a city, it did not exist at all. The small sloops that moored at the river's edge to unload their cargo did not dock at Hudson, but at what had for many years been known as Claverack Landing. Two small wharves and two small stone storehouses serviced the sloops that brought goods to the landing to exchange for produce from the farms of Claverack, a community settled by the Dutch in the seventeenth century and located a few miles inland from the river.

Before the Dutch arrived, Claverack Landing was part of the vast domain of the Mahicans (or Mohicans, as they are known today), who were the original inhabitants of this part of New York State. For hundreds of years before the arrival of Europeans, the Mohicans were masters of an area that included the land south of what is now Lake Champlain, west to the Schoharie Creek, east to Vermont and New Hampshire, and south to Manhattan Island. Living, as many of the tribes did, along the banks of the Hudson River (which they called Mahicannituck), they named themselves Muh-he-con-neok, "the People of the Waters That Are Never Still."

In 1609 a small ship, unlike anything the Mohicans had ever seen, sailed up the great river. The ship carried only a handful of men—nothing as compared to the numbers of those into whose lands it had come. But small as it was, tiny against the immensity of the river it rode upon and dwarfed next to the dark and immeasurable vastness of the forests that covered the shores, the effect of its arrival would be monumental, and for the Mohicans ultimately catastrophic. Whatever else was in its hold, it carried a fatal destiny for the native people. Its arrival augured the end of the Mohicans' sway over their ancient land.

The Great River of the Mountains: Henry Hudson in 1609

It was in March of 1609 that Henry Hudson, an Englishman exploring for the Dutch East India Company in search of a passage that would lead to the riches of the East Indies, sailed from Amsterdam in the *Half Moon*, a small and ungainly ship of about sixty tons with a crew of twenty—a mix of English and Dutch sailors, most of whom did not speak the other's language. By the end of May, Hudson had arrived in Nova Scotia. He traveled on to the coast of Maine, entering Penobscot Bay on July 18. On July 26 he sailed south and arrived in late August at Chesapeake Bay and then Delaware Bay. Convinced that there was no passage to be found there to the Pacific and the Indies, he turned northward again, sailing up the coast. Finally he entered what would one day be called the Bay of New York. Into it flowed a huge river from the north. To Hudson, it seemed possible that this might be the passage he was seeking.

On September 12 he began his journey up the river. By September 14 he came to West Point, and by September 15 he began to see the high bluffs and headlands that distinguish the riverbank—the same scenes that two centuries later would become the romantic subject of the Hudson River School of painters. On the evening of September 15, Hudson anchored off the site of modern-day Catskill, where he recorded in his journal that he had made contact with local inhabitants, whom he described as "very loving people" who helped him stock his ship with "Indian corn, pumpkins and tobacco."

The next day, September 16, 1609, Hudson anchored somewhere between Stockport and the site of modern-day Hudson. There he was again visited by local inhabitants—Algonquin-speaking Mohicans—and returned to shore with them. Hudson wrote of the encounter:

> I sailed to the shore in one of their canoes with an old man who was Chief of a tribe consisting of forty men and seventeen women. These I saw there in a house well constructed of oak bark, and circular in shape, so that it had the appearance of being built with an arched roof. It contained a great quantity of Indian corn and beans of the last year's growth, and there lay near the house for purpose of drying enough to load a ship.
>
> On our coming into the house two mats were spread out to sit upon, and some food was immediately served in well made red wooden bowls. Two men were also dispatched at once with bows and arrows in quest of game, who soon returned with a pair of pigeons which they had shot. They likewise killed a fat dog, and skinned it in great haste with shells which they had got out of the water.
>
> They supposed that I should remain with them the night, but I returned after a short time on board the ship. These are a very good people for when they saw I would not remain with them, they supposed that I was afraid of their bows, and taking their arrows, they broke them in pieces and threw them in the fire.[2]

It cannot be ascertained whether this house "well constructed of oak bark, and circular in shape" was located in the city of Hudson. Excavations made at the foot of Warren Street in the eighteenth or early nineteenth century revealed what Anna Bradbury, author of *History of the City of Hudson, N.Y.,* described in 1908 as "the unmistakable remains of an Indian village." Given the latitude recorded for the ship's location in 1609, however, it is more likely that the chief's lodge was located somewhere near the mouth of Stockport Creek, a few miles north of Hudson.

On September 17, Hudson left his hosts and sailed farther up the river that he called the River of the Mountains and that one day would be named after him. Hudson came to the present site of Albany on September 18. On September 23, Hudson began his voyage back downriver, and on September 24 his ship ran aground "on a bank of ooze in the middle of the river." It would be two days before he was able to float the ship again. During this time the *Half Moon* was approached by two canoes carrying Mohicans. Among them was a chief whose lordly ways suggested that he was master of all the land around. This chief gave Hudson presents of belts of wampum. Invited to dine aboard ship, the chief arrived with two old women and "two young maidens of the age of sixteen or seventeen who behaved themselves very modestly." For the next two days Hudson restocked his ship with food and wood and explored the shores. On September 27, amid protestations of sorrow from the Mohicans and with assurances that he would return, Hudson set sail, leaving behind the place that would one day bear his name.[3]

As he proceeded up and then back down the river, which early maps of the New World called variously Riviere Vendome, Rio de Guames, Rio San Antonio, the Great River, Manhattan, Mauritius, Nassau, Noorden Kill, Groote Kill, and Noordt Rivier (or North River), and which the Mohicans alternately called Shatemuc, Hudson noted in his journal how impressed he was by the fertility and beauty of the landscape, observing that "the land is the finest for cultivation that I ever in life set foot upon" and that "it is as beautiful land as ever one can tread upon, abounding in walnut, chestnut, yew and trees of sweet wood in abundance."

A Parcel of Land
Lying in the Klaverack:
Claverack Landing, 1662–1784

The qualities noted by Henry Hudson soon drew Dutch settlers to the Hudson River Valley. Jan Frans Van Hoesen, attracted by the beauty of the landscape, the river frontage, the amount and value of its timber, and its fertile inland soil ripe for cultivation, purchased from the Mohicans in 1662 a large tract of land that included the present area of Hudson and what is now Greenport and Stockport. The Van Hoesen land was bounded by the river

Map of Claverack Landing (1774) before the arrival of the Proprietors, showing the wharves of Colonel John Van Alen and Peter Hogeboom, Jr. Courtesy of the Office of the Columbia County Clerk, Hudson, New York.

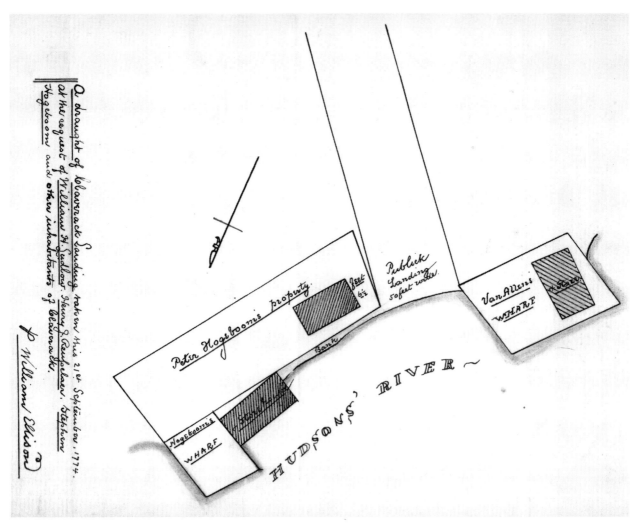

and extended inland to beyond Claverack Creek. Its boundaries provided its name, for it was land that encompassed three of the *klavers* (Dutch for "cliffs") that rose on the river-bank and the rack ("reach," or distance) between them. The land was identified as that "lying in the Klaverack on the east side of the river."[4]

A road was built, certainly only a rough dirt track, which everyone called the "waggon-way." It extended from a wharf on the river landing and roughly followed the present Allen Street to Partition Street, then across what is now Seventh Street Park, and thence to the farms of Claverack.

Van Hoesen farmed his land for almost forty years. When he died in 1703, the land went to his son, Jurrien Van Hoesen, who subsequently divided it among his two brothers, Jacob and Johannes, and his sister, Catherine, who had married Francis Herdyk (or Hardick). The Hardick land was north of the "waggon-way"; Johannes Van Hoesen's was to the south. The two parcels included the area of the present city of Hudson, and on this land a settlement began to grow.

The census of 1714 shows that 219 people lived in the settlement, and sixteen of them were slaves. Probably in the late 1730s, Hardick sold some of his land to Jeremiah Hogeboom, who built a "store and a wharf" on the river. Though other structures no doubt had been built there, this is the first recorded mention of buildings in the settlement of Claverack Landing.

Hogeboom's store, or storehouse, stood at the river's edge at the base of State Street. It was eventually joined by a warehouse on a site at the corner of Ferry and Water Street, as a map of 1774 shows. This warehouse was built by Colonel John Van Alen, who had married into the Van Hoesen family. Nearby was Van Alen's house, one of the largest of the settlement, built of brick with high gables and high entry steps (which the Dutch called a *stoep*). There was a ferry slip at the river's edge under the management of Conradt Flaack, who took people across to Lunenburgh (now Athens) in a canoe.

For many years Claverack Landing remained a quiet settlement, a port for small sloops and for traders who carried local goods up and down the river. Local settlers brought cab-bages and cattle, flax and hemp, herring, produce, and grain to the landing to be traded for cloth, tools, and other necessities brought upriver from New York City. Even during the uncertain times of the French and Indian wars of the 1750s, Claverack Landing remained relatively untroubled, untouched by skirmishes or attacks. In 1774 when the Revolutionary War came, the people of the landing raised a regiment, the First Claverack Battalion, com-manded by Lieutenant Colonel Johannes Van Hoesen. Van Hoesens, Hogebooms, Hardicks, Esseltyns, and Huycks are mentioned as answering their country's call.

Claverack Landing was a seemingly inconsequential place, but it stood in an unrivaled position. Its long and easily accessible waterfront was protected by the island on which some believed that Hudson's ship had run aground. Just to the south lay a large, beautiful bay, and on the north lay another, equally impressive bay. The river in front of the landing was deep enough even for oceangoing vessels to dock close to shore. The forests nearby had plentiful timber, perfect for building ships. All of this would conjure visions of a safe har-bor and busy commerce for those with the imagination to see it.

Concerned with Navigating the Deep:
The Proprietors, 1783–1784

In 1774 the Continental Congress suspended all trade with England. The British retaliated by attacking and destroying American shipping whenever possible. Among American ships destroyed were many owned by New England whalers. The loss of ships and crews who were killed or captured in these attacks was a near-fatal blow to the industry. Then, when Britain imposed a prohibitive tariff on whale oil, the whaler's profits were reduced to virtually nothing. So severe were the losses in ships and men, and so damaged was the market for their product that Nantucket, which at the time of the Revolutionary War was the largest whaling station in the world, went into a decline from which many of the merchants there doubted it would recover.

A group of these beleaguered merchants—most of whom derived their livelihood from the sea and were Quakers from Nantucket, Providence, Newport, and Martha's Vineyard—determined to seek new business opportunities elsewhere. In the spring of 1783, they formed an association, the purpose of which was to find a place to start afresh and make new homes for their families. The association was conceived and led by Thomas Jenkins, one of the wealthiest merchants among them. Jenkins was a native of Nantucket, but had become a resident of Providence. The new association consisted of thirty members, all of whom were merchants or those "concerned with navigating the deep." Their surnames would become familiar in early Hudson history: Alsop, Paddock, Clark, Greene, Thurston, Coffin, Worth, Macy, Allen, Morgan, and of course Jenkins. In fact, the Jenkins family contributed six members to the association, including its only female member, Deborah Jenkins. The association decided that the place to look for their new safe haven would be on the Hudson River.

In the summer of 1783, four members of the association—Thomas Jenkins, Cotton Gelston, possibly Thomas's brother Seth, and an unnamed fourth—were sent to the Hudson to scout locations for the new enterprise. Their voyage was not an odyssey of discovery to chart new lands, but a cool appraisal of available real estate on a river familiar to them and to most merchant seamen of the time. They began in New York City, where they considered a tract of land on the East River, but they decided that the parcel was too small and too expensive. Poughkeepsie attracted them next, but there, too, nothing seemed right. Proceeding upriver, they finally came to the little sloop landing at Claverack Landing, which was the furthest upriver that ships of deep draught could go. There they saw what they were looking for: deep-water docking, easy access to the river, and a landing where two warehouses had already been built and were profitable mercantile concerns. Above the riverbank, high on a bluff, there was a site on which to build a city—for it was a city they intended to build. On either side of the site were two enormous bays (in Dutch called the Norder Bought and Souder Bought—North Bay and South Bay). Neither bay was deep enough for large ships, but both offered land on their shores with large stands of timber fit for development. Broad and fertile land, fruitful and already profitably farmed, stretched out in every direction from the bays.

They did not hesitate. On July 19, 1783, Thomas Jenkins, acting for the association, purchased the wharf and warehouse belonging to Peter Hogeboom for £2,600. A few days later the Hardicks sold their lands—all the area lying north of today's Partition Street and

The Penfield Map of the city of Hudson (1799), showing the street grid laid out by the Proprietors. Collection of the Columbia County Historical Society, Kinderhook, New York.

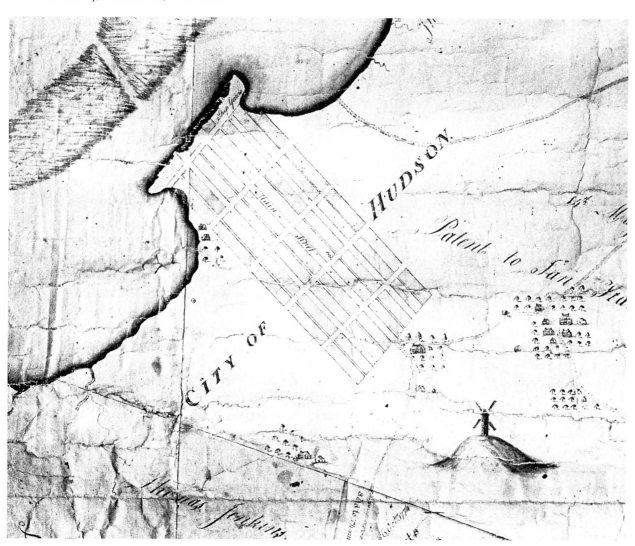

extending to the North Bay—for £2,340. In September some twelve acres—the tract bounded by today's Second and Mill streets—was purchased from another member of the Hardick family for £250. Within a few weeks the last of the land was sold to Jenkins: first, the holdings of Colonel John Van Alen for £2,500, which included most of the waterfront and lands around the present Ferry Street; then, Van Hoesen land east of today's Front Street and below the "waggon way"; and finally, land belonging to Casper Huyck east of the Van Hoesen tract. In just a few months time the purchase of Claverack Landing was complete. Jenkins and the association, which now called itself the Proprietors, had bought it all for somewhere in the neighborhood of £10,000—well over $1 million in today's currency.

By that fall, three of the new proprietors of Hudson had arrived with their families and possessions to join Thomas Jenkins and Cotton Gelston. These were Seth Jenkins (Thomas Jenkins's brother), John Alsop, and Joseph Barnard. They came from Providence on the brig *Comet,* captained by Eleazer Jenkins. Seth Jenkins and Alsop lived aboard the *Comet* until their houses were completed near the riverbank. Barnard built his house on the site that would become the northeast corner of First and Main (Warren) streets, while another of the Barnard clan built a house farther up the road, between what would become First and Second streets. These were the first houses built in the new settlement.

Others arrived in the spring of 1784. Jared Coffin's family came on the schooner *Joseph,* on which they lived while their house was being built on what would be Union Street, opposite First. Some, like Stephen Paddock, brought along houses that were already partially built—houses framed in Providence or Nantucket and ready for raising. Paddock raised his on a lot near the river on what was soon to be North Front Street. He lived there until he bought the new house built by Robert Barnard on the corner of First and Main.

It might have been expected that the new proprietors, as recent arrivals and as the moneyed new owners of the old settlement, would be received by the old residents with hostility and even suspicion. But the day of Paddock's arrival, he was greeted by a "stout and fine looking gentleman, evidently of Dutch descent, wearing a scarlet coat." This was Colonel Van Alen, the leader of the small community. Van Alen welcomed the Paddocks and invited them to dine and stay with him until their own house was ready. "If he is a sample of my new neighbors," Paddock is said to have remarked, "then we are in a happy land."[5] Indeed, despite some opposition from residents of more distant Kinderhook and the countryside of Claverack, relations were cordial between the newcomers and the old families—the Ten Broecks, Delamaters, Huycks, Millers, and Hogebooms.

The Proprietors had their first meeting on May 14, 1784. A committee of six was appointed to "regulate the streets and to attend in a particular manner to the fixings [i.e., the site] of the buildings uniformly." They were so fond of uniformity that they further voted that "no person should fix his house without direction from a majority of the committee and that no person should extend his steps more than four feet from his front door."

An early map of the as yet unbuilt city shows the design. Four main streets (later named Union, Main [Warren], Diamond [Columbia], and State) ran uptown from the river and were fronted with large, uniform building lots. Behind these were twenty-foot-wide alleys running parallel to the main streets. Intersecting the main streets were four cross streets on what are now Front, Second, Third, and Fourth streets. (The present First Street was actually created some years later.)

The streets were mostly rough dirt roads. Some, like Front Street, were dug and sometimes blasted out of rock. Main Street, running from the river to Prospect Hill, was nearly level until it reached midway between Third and Fourth, where a deep hollow cut across it. There the road was so narrow that there was barely room for even one cart or wagon, and it was so low that the entrances to the houses were many feet above it, forcing people to walk a plank to get into their homes. Farther along, at Fourth, there was an even deeper hollow. Above Fourth, the road ran precariously along a ridge with deep ravines on either side. This is where the businesses of the 500 and 600 blocks of Warren Street can now be found, but in the 1780s there were no buildings save for the single small store of the presumably optimistic Isaac Northrup, which stood on the corner of North Fifth and Main. Above Northrup's store, midway up the street, was another deep and dangerous gully. Sidewalks were sometimes paved with large stones or with planks laid in the dirt, but more often they were just bare ground. When it rained, these dirt sidewalks became so impassable that it was said that "it cost two shillings to get a woman out of the mud."

Progress without Parallel: Hudson in 1785

During the next year the Proprietors entered into a number of projects. They hired people to "dig on the hill" in the direction of Main in order to open a way to the river, thus opening South Front Street. They built a market house 20 feet by 30 feet in size at the northwest corner of Front and Main. The space adjoining it became Market Square. They decided that the "great hollow" in Main Street at Fourth should be spanned by a bridge "with stone abutments." They brought water into the city, first from a spring given to them by John Ten Broeck, and then from a "fountain" on the road between Claverack and Hudson. The water was brought into the city by an aqueduct—a wooden pipe— that ran down Main Street. Each lot holder could take water from the aqueduct for a fee, and the town pump was located at Market Square. Water could be taken from the pump at six in the morning, at noon, and again at five in the evening. The Proprietors also proposed a school for Market Square and began to build a city hall, a plain two-story brick building on the corner of Warren and Fourth where the First Presbyterian Church now stands.

The Proprietors had made such a success of their venture that by 1784, Claverack Landing was the second most active port in New York State. Seagoing ships brought goods from Europe, while fast-sailing river sloops brought merchandise from New York City and carried Hudson's goods back downriver. On November 14, 1784, in a gesture both to the river and to its discoverer, the Proprietors changed the name of their burgeoning settlement to Hudson.

Just a few months later, in 1785, the city of Hudson was chartered. And a city, indeed, it was. The ten or so families—no more than one hundred persons—and the handful of dwellings that the Proprietors had seen upon their first arrival in 1783 had grown astoundingly. By the end of 1786, more than 150 dwellings, as well as wharves, barns, shops, and warehouses, had been built. The population, according to an issue of the *New York Journal,* was more than 1,500 people.

GOING SHOPPING: MAIN STREET IN 1785

It must have been exhilarating. Businesses reflected the new prosperity and the growing sophistication of Hudson's inhabitants. Most of the businesses were on Main Street below Third Street, or on Front Street. Thomas Jenkins sold "the best West India and New England Rum, Iron, Salt and Dry Goods" near the dock, as did the firm of Green and Mansfield. John Bolles was a saddler next door to Jenkins, and Richard Bowles plied the same trade nearby. On Main Street could be found merchant Cotton Gelston's store, as well as the store of Dr. Levi Wheaton, one of the first physicians in Hudson, selling "drugs and medicines." If Dr. Wheaton's stock of drugs was insufficient, more could be found at a shop run by Quaker patriarch, Lot Tripp.

Shubael Worth, a general merchant, was at the corner of Main and Second streets. Walter Johnson, "from Newport," was a baker at the corner of Front and Ferry streets, and Mrs. Newberry, whose gingerbread was famous, made cakes and buns in her house and shop on Front Street. The ladies could peruse "silk and shoes for sale" at the shop of Thomas Worth "near the market," and if Mr. Worth's shoes did not suit, then Gideon Talbot, boot and shoemaker, could provide. Having bought their cloth, the ladies might have it made into the latest fashions at the shop of J. Pritchard, "from London," who was a "Taylor and Ladies Habit-maker." If Pritchard would not do, they could have the work done at the shop of Phineas June or by Mrs. Hussey. Mrs. Hussey was "happy to wait upon the ladies at her house on the hill near the wharf," where she could create "the most approved fashions regularly received from New York." Both women and men could be outfitted at the shop of Dennis Macnemara, "Taylor for Ladies and Gentlemen."

Mr. Hyacinth Lescure, lately from France, offered "a choice lot of essences near the Market House" as well as "cushions to the ladies and queues to the gentlemen of excellent human hair." Mr. James Robardet of Connecticut set himself up as "an instructor in the polite accomplishments of dancing." T. R. Bowles ran a general store, Mr. Dilworth sold "spelling books by the Dozen or single," and all of this activity was celebrated—and advertised—in Hudson's first newspaper, the *Hudson Weekly Gazette,* printed by the firm of Webster and Stoddard. The first issue was published on April 7, 1785, wherein one Philo Socius protested in a letter that Robardet's dancing school would be sure to "send all the young people of the city directly to perdition."

Bunker and Easton were tanners. Latham Bunker was a blacksmith. Tristram and Brazillai Bunker made sails, as did Seth Jenkins and Stephen Paddock on Third Street. Ropes were made by Josiah Olcott and Thomas Jenkins on a "rope walk" near Third Street north of State Street (where Rope Alley is today). The five shipyards were one of Hudson's leading industries. Between 1785 and 1800, thirty-two ships were built in the city, and city merchants owned twenty-five ships.[6] Both Obed Sears and John T. Lacy built ships, as did Titus Morgan, whose yard was at the foot of State Street.

The first seagoing vessel built in the city, a huge ship of three hundred tons called the *Hudson,* was launched in 1785 by the firm of Jenkins and Gelston. That launch was an occasion for a public festival. Schools were closed, country folk came into the city, shops were shuttered, and the whole city trooped down to the yards to see the huge ship slide into the river, outfitted with the city's own sails, ropes, and tackle. Standing on the riverbank, Hudsonians enjoyed the carnival atmosphere. Munching on the famed gingerbread made by the formidable Mrs. Newberry, they waited for the ship to move. When it did, guns were fired and cheers were raised, more gingerbread was consumed, and toasts perhaps were proposed in Hudson Ale, made by Benjamin Faulkins at his brewery near the river.

Hudsonians also drank the beer and ale brewed near the market by David Cooper. Mr. Auchmoody made his brew on Cherry Alley between Fourth and Fifth. Hudson beer and liquor was, in fact, quite famous. The *New York Journal* opined that one of Hudson's distilleries was "one of the best distilleries in America." Obviously the production of liquor and beer was profitable. The pious but practical Quakers licensed a large number of firms, many of which were owned by the Quakers themselves, to "retail all kinds of spirituous liquors." In fact, the mayor, four members of the common council, and fifteen of the original Proprietors were engaged in the liquor trade.

The city had much to celebrate, and the number of taverns in the city indicates that there were many places in which to do it. In 1786 there were nineteen innkeepers licensed in Hudson. The first tavern in Hudson, marked by a sign bearing the head of the King of Prussia, was opened by Colonel John McKinstry in the 200 block of Warren Street. Hudson was a convivial town. Three hundred Hudsonians attended a Fourth of July celebration in 1785 where thirteen toasts—to the fair sex, to liberty, and so on—were offered. The city welcomed visitors with equally bibulous celebrations. John Jay came to town in 1792 and was treated to an elegant dinner at Kellogg's Tavern, where eleven toasts were proposed. In 1824 the Marquis de Lafayette stopped in Hudson long enough to be grandly feted by the people with parades and festooned streets, at the head of which a huge statue of the Goddess of Liberty was erected. Sitting on a throne at the courthouse, Lafayette was toasted repeatedly, and while he was unable to stay for the dinner that had been prepared for him, all of Hudson's high society turned out and the celebration went on into the night.[7]

KEEPING THE SABBATH: HUDSON'S FIRST CHURCHES

Respectable Hudson was a churchgoing town, though "among the seafaring portion of the population were to be found many who belonged to no particular church and consequently paid tribute to none."[8] The Proprietors were predominantly Quakers, and at the time, probably two-thirds of Hudson's residents were Quakers, so a meetinghouse was deemed an early necessity for the new settlement. The Proprietors gave the Society of Friends (the Quakers' official name) a lot on Union Street just a few doors up from the corner of Third, upon which they built a frame meetinghouse and school in 1784. This soon proved too small for their numbers. In 1794 they bought a lot at the corner of Union and Third (the current site of the Hudson Boys and Girls Club) and built a simple and spare brick building devoid of ornament—as was their style and taste—but large enough to hold 600 people.

The Quakers were strict in their observances, which were simple to the point of starkness. "There is no regular service, no reading, no praying, no singing, and nine Sundays out of ten, there is even no preaching and consequently the whole broad-brimmed and dove colored flock sit together in profound silence for three mortal hours!"[9] Neglecting to attend meeting or sleeping during it, wearing anything but the

plainest clothes, reading books that were considered by the elders to be pernicious, mar-
rying outside of the Society of Friends, or frequenting taverns were all cause for disci-
pline. The Friends kept themselves separate from the "world's people," as they called their
non-Quaker neighbors, but they were not otherworldly. While they did not value the
trinkets of the world for their personal use, they were shrewd businessmen and struck
hard bargains when they sought to buy those trinkets or to sell them to others.

As Hudson's mercantile endeavors declined, and as its men went less and less to sea,
so its Quakers—merchants and seamen almost all—declined in numbers also. The
Quakers, responsible for the city's founding, comprised most of the population of
Hudson in its first years and were the mainstays of its trade and society for a century.
By the late nineteenth century, however, orthodox Quakers numbered only twelve in
their meeting and the Hicksite Friends (a large faction within the Quaker community)
numbered only a few more.[10] Few Quakers can be seen in Hudson today, but the
heritage the Quakers left is all around—in the houses they built and in the city they
imagined and brought to life. If spirits survive, then Hudson must surely be haunted by
thrifty Quakers, perhaps even now soberly and busily going about their affairs in the
shadow world.

Presbyterians were the second-largest denomination in the city after the Quakers.
They had been worshipping in the as yet unfinished city hall on the corner of Warren
and Fourth Street, but by 1790 the congregation had become large enough to warrant
building a church of its own. By 1792 they had finished constructing a plain brick
building, which was the first church (as opposed to a Quaker meetinghouse) to be
erected in Hudson. The church was located on Second Street between Partition Street
and Allen Street (at the time called Federal Street). The brick building was topped with
a tall steeple with a weathervane. Anyone vigorous enough to climb to the top of the
steeple could have glorious views of the South Bay, the river, and the mountains. In the
steeple was a bell that was rung by one Jemmy Fraser at morning, noon, and at night
on working days, and to call worshippers to church on the Sabbath. The Presbyterians
were a sober lot, but they apparently were tolerant. Their bell-ringer had a reputation
for being fond of frequenting Hudson's taverns, a fondness which a few years later cost
the hapless Fraser his next position as Hudson's town crier, a position that ended with
his dismissal.

The other two Protestant denominations to build churches in Hudson in the
eighteenth century were the Methodists and the Episcopalians. The Methodists had met
for some years in a private home on Cherry Alley near Front Street. In 1790 they built
a frame church able to seat 200 people on what is now the southeast corner of Third
and Diamond Street, adjoining Prison Alley.

Christ Church Episcopal was the fourth and last church established in Hudson in the
eighteenth century. Originally meeting for worship in the schoolhouse on Diamond
Street, the Episcopalians began to build on the southeast corner of Second and State
streets in 1795. It took several years to complete construction; the church was finally consecrated in 1803.

None of the Protestant churches built in Hudson in the eighteenth century remain.
The oldest house of worship in the city is the small Quaker meetinghouse on Union
Street below Fourth, a simple remnant of a vanished time.[11]

KEEPING THE PEACE: LAWS AND ORDER

Now that they had a city with a mayor (Seth Jenkins) and a governing council (though many of the council were also Proprietors, and the Proprietors still owned Hudson), the city fathers moved to regulate the city by passing laws, defining crimes, and meting out punishments. In 1785, Hudson's first prison—the "gaol," a one-story log building about 30 feet by 15 feet with grates on the doors and windows—was erected across from city hall on the corner of Fourth Street and Prison Alley. Its first prisoner is said to have gained his freedom by boring through the wooden walls with an auger that he had somehow obtained.

Presuming that the rigors of corporal punishment might be more effective in deterring crime than imprisonment, it was soon decided that a stocks and whipping post should be erected at Market Square. The whipping post was precisely that—a heavy post set deeply into the ground. Culprits convicted of petty offenses were tied to it and received on their bare back the number of lashes deemed by the judge to be appropriate to the offense. The *Hudson Weekly Gazette* for August 1787 reported that "John Bennett, alias William Smith, was convicted in this city for stealing a canoe and received thirty-nine stripes at the public post."[12] More hardened criminals were tied behind a horse-drawn cart that proceeded slowly up Main Street from the lower end of town. The criminal received a certain number of lashes at each corner, administered by a city official called the whipping master. When the head of Main Street was reached, the offender was freed and sternly told to leave the city forever.

A disapproving eye was cast by the pious Quaker Proprietors upon various forms of misbehavior. A committee was appointed to "superintend the execution of the law against Sabbath breaking." No meat was to be sold after eight in the morning on Sundays, and barber shops were to be shut by ten. Breaking the peace of the Sabbath, rowdiness, and vagrancy were all subject to penalties. Anyone who "galloped his, her or their horses through the streets of the city" was fined six shillings, one half to go to the "Overseers of the Poor" and the other to the person who informed on the illegal galloper. Shopkeepers could not throw glass in the streets, no one could "chop wood on Main Street with an axe," and anyone who allowed any "hog or hogs, goose or geese" to run without being "properly yoked" could also be fined. High-spirited youth seemed to especially disturb the Quaker peace. Boys were forbidden to swim near the ferry landing, and in an effort to control boyish rowdiness the Proprietors passed ordinances forbidding ball playing and hoop rolling on Main Street. But boys will, as was no doubt said, be boys, and the unlighted streets were ideal for their hijinks. Stoops were sometimes overturned, gates were unhinged, and signs were misplaced or stolen. The press complained that the "disgraceful course of certain young men" must be curbed to prevent such nighttime depredations.

Robberies were frequent. Such was the public concern that in 1788 the council created the Hudson night watch. These were volunteers who could interrogate, and confine until the next day if they chose, any citizen who was out too late or who appeared suspicious. The night watch were armed with heavy clubs with which they sounded the hours by blows upon posts, and presumably subdued any recalcitrant suspicious persons who resisted confinement. It was probably the fear of robberies that led the council to place twenty oil lamps in the streets in 1797, and a lamplighter was hired to light them at nightfall (but not upon moonlit nights).

City records show that the Proprietors were dubious about the moral character of single or abandoned women: "Whereas John Dewitt, late of the City of New York has run away and left his wife and children in Hudson, it is ordered that Mrs. Dewitt, with her children be sent to the city of New York." To join her absconded husband, or just to get her out of town? More charitably (perhaps) the Overseers of the Poor were authorized to give $2.50 per month to Phoebe Cummings if she would take herself and her children out of the city. What had Cummings done to deserve banishment?

Franklin Ellis, the author of *History of Columbia County,* observed in a brief aside on the moral climate of late-eighteenth-century Hudson that when the trim sloop with the racy name *Free Love* landed at Hudson wharf, it did not cause "moral people to look askance at the community which was settling here" as it might have done a few decades later, for "in those days the name carried no evil significance and produced no unjust suspicions."[13] Moral people *did* look askance on certain Hudson residents, for in 1787 the Proprietors made it clear that there was no welcome for one Freelove Clark. She was ordered to return to Nantucket, and Stephen Paddock was sternly authorized to take whatever measures were necessary to remove her from the city. Stephen B. Miller, in his 1862 *Sketches of Hudson,* delicately suggests that Freelove Clark was banished because it was the city custom to send "vagrants" back to their places of residence.[14]

Is the term "vagrant" meant to suggest that Freelove Clark was a prostitute? Bruce Hall, in *Diamond Street: The Story of the Little Town with the Big Red Light District,* argues that prostitutes may have arrived in Hudson in the same year that the Proprietors were founding it. During the Revolutionary War, the British provided prostitutes for their troops in encampments in New York City. In 1783, when America triumphed, the "brazen harlots," as Hall says, "were driven out of town by the victorious Americans" and found their way to upstate towns. Whether any came to Hudson, we do not know. Hall speculates that because many "sailors and merchants and other travelers passed through Hudson in the early days" and because Hudson was well-stocked with taverns, there "were plenty of working girls available … to show a drunken sailor a good time." He further conjectures that the Proprietors may not have frowned on such carnal generosity because "the Proprietors wanted to make sure the clientele was happy."[15] Whether they indeed took such a genial, tolerant, and pragmatic view of the economic benefits that might come from vice in Hudson, no records show. All that we know is that unhappy Freelove Clark fell under their stern eye and her activities merited summary banishment.

Fire was a constant threat. In 1793 the bookstore and printing office of Ashbel Stoddard caught fire. A contemporary account dryly notes: "The organization of the fire department being extremely deficient, there being no engines, no buckets, no water and no firemen, the fire was left to take its course."[16] A group of citizens circulated a subscription to buy a fire engine that would have four pumps and good enough suction to throw water up to 300 feet. The group petitioned the council to allow them to form themselves into a fire company. Soon a second group did the same, and by 1794 Hudson had two fire companies—the forerunners of Hudson's volunteer fire companies that still exist to this day and which are the oldest volunteer fire companies in America.

Other precautions were taken against fire. Every owner of a house with three fireplaces was required to keep near the door two leather buckets marked with his initials and sufficient to hold two gallons of water. Four-fireplace homes needed three buckets, and bakers and tavern keepers were directed to have buckets large enough to hold three gallons each. Fire wardens were appointed. At the first sign of fire, their job was to form Hudsonians—women and men—into bucket brigades and direct them through a speaking trumpet. Upon hearing the cry of "Fire!" inhabitants were instructed to put lighted candles in their windows to help illuminate the dark streets, and to throw their buckets into the street so that fire wardens could get them quickly. The mayor and aldermen were to be in attendance at the conflagration, equipped with five-foot-long white wands with gilded flames at the tip.

SELF-IMPROVEMENT:
SCHOOLS, LIBRARIES, AND NEWSPAPERS

Having created a rudimentary police force and a fire company, the next wave of Hudson self-improvement came in the form of libraries, schools, and newspapers, established with varying degrees of success. Claverack Landing had provided early on for the schooling of its children. Records show that a school had been built even before the Proprietors arrived. This school stood near the river, perhaps near the corner of the present Partition and Ferry streets (that is, on the old "waggon way"). It was attended in 1784 by children of both the Proprietors and the Dutch, and the teacher was James Burns. Hudson's first teacher has left no record of his labors, but it was said that he was a careful and prudent man, and quickly sent the children home whenever it became clear that workmen opening the road down to the river were about to set off blasting charges. In fact, opening the street led to the demolition of Hudson's first schoolhouse sometime after 1785.

The Proprietors agreed that they would donate a 40-by-24-foot lot on Diamond Street to anyone who would build a school. It was stipulated that no class or denomination should be excluded from this school. Who built it is not known, and who went there is unrecorded, but it is known that Joseph Marshall announced that he would hold classes there and offered an extensive and grueling curriculum consisting of "reading, writing, ciphering, composition, English grammar, geography, surveying, and the Latin and Greek languages."[17] The new school was open to all (to all who could pay, that is), but that egalitarian foundation may have made some of the exclusive Quakers fearful of the dangers attendant upon allowing their children to be taught in too-intimate proximity with "people of the world." Just a few weeks later, a proposal went before the Proprietors to build a Proprietors' school on Market Square.

It is not known if that school was built. Nor is it known whether Ambrose Liverpool, who had enterprisingly announced in the *Hudson Weekly Gazette* that he could teach English, Latin, and Greek as well as the "principles of several musical instruments," actually opened a school or not, though some might have had second thoughts about a teacher who revealed in the same advertisement that he had "several dozen casks of strong English beer which he wished to dispose of." Schools opened where teachers lived or could rent space for their classrooms. Major Fowler taught at his house on

Parade Alley. Another in-home school was taught near the saddlery of Mr. Burns. Mr. Hedge had a school in the west chamber of city hall, while Mr. Palmer ran a school in the east chamber. None of these, of course, were free; teachers earned their keep from the payments made by students. There is no way to know the quality of the education given or the nature of what was taught, but an editorial in 1806 describing the state of education before the opening of the Hudson Academy in 1807 suggests that all was not entirely well in Hudson's little academic community:

> No public building for the education of youth had been built in the city of Hudson. No public encouragement was given to literary pursuits. The citizens of the most flourishing town in the state were compelled to send their children abroad for education or to leave them uneducated. If a teacher appeared among them, he had everything to discourage him. He had to procure his rooms, obtain his scholars, and collect his own subscriptions.

Indeed, no one seemed to think that education was necessary. The Common Council in 1803 appropriated the "money now in the hands of the treasurer" for schools and reassigned it for an unspecified "contingent purpose." There had been no provision made for free education in Hudson, and there would be none until 1841.[18]

If education was in such a parlous state, it may be no wonder that Hudson's libraries did not fare all that well either. The first library may have opened in 1786 and been run from the store and printing office of Ashbel Stoddard, who had begun the city's first newspaper in 1785. It is known that Stoddard kept a bookstore in his shop as well, and this might have been the first library. The store was destroyed in Hudson's first major fire in 1793.

The Columbia Library was formed soon after, and its collection may have been kept in Stoddard's rebuilt store. The Hudson Library Society, which might have been an off-shoot of the Columbia Library, appeared around 1797 and was believed to have been located in a back room of the store of Shubael Worth on the northwest corner of Warren and Second Street. It would appear, however, that Hudson was more interested in trade than in books, for the Hudson Library Society barely limped along until it finally closed for lack of interest and lack of funds, even though the cost of subscribing was not high. One of the early libraries advertised that subscriptions could be purchased for four dollars per year (about seventy-five dollars today) and books could be borrowed at the rate of two cents per day.

But people did want to know the news. Hudson's first newspaper, the *Hudson Weekly Gazette,* printed and published by Ashbel Stoddard at the corner of Warren and Third Street, appeared in 1785. Stoddard also published the *Columbian Almanac,* which was said to reliably predict the weather, and the *Columbian Magazine,* a literary and social journal with religious leanings, which failed after a year. The *Hudson Weekly Gazette* cost twelve shillings per year, was about eight-by-ten-inches in size, and was printed on coarse, yellowish paper. The paper was delivered to each subscriber by a young man who announced his arrival by blowing loudly on a horn. Readers may have been unhappy with its first few issues, for there was little advertising, but eventually the *Gazette* caught on. Hyacinth Lescure became an advertiser, announcing that he would accept payment in "wheat or

Indian corn" for the cushions and queues of human hair that he could furnish to ladies and gentlemen. Slaves were also for sale in the *Gazette's* pages, as one 1785 ad illustrates: "For sale a likely Negro wench about 30 years of age. Also a Negro child one year and a half old." Another advertisement read, "To be sold: several Negroes for cash." Hudson's Quakers were opposed to slavery and tried without success to abolish it in Hudson. The *Hudson Weekly Gazette* announced in May 1785 that "a number of citizens" had formed themselves into a society for promoting the manumission of slaves "and protecting such of them as have been or may be liberated."[19]

During the next decades Hudson saw a number of newspapers come and go (the *Hudson Weekly Gazette* closed about 1804). Most were politically oriented papers, supporting various parties and factions. The *Balance* was the Federal paper, while the *Bee* was the voice of anti-Federalism. The *Republican Fountain* supported a faction of the Democratic Party. The *Northern Whig* had Federalist sympathies, as did the *Columbia Republican*. The *Gazette* was a Democratic paper. The *Magnolia*, the *Diamond*, and the *Flail and the Thresher* were all political, while the *Columbia Washingtonian* called for temperance. Hudson's first daily papers, the *Hudson Daily Star* and the *Evening Register*, are the ancestors of Hudson's current daily, the *Register-Star*.

The times prompted debate on many vital issues, but the primary subject of debate in the newspapers and in the debating societies (the Hudson Union Debating Society was founded in 1786) was politics. People formed into factions, and Hudson had political clubs that served as social clubs as well. Federalism versus anti-Federalism was the primary political issue. The Anti-Federalists numbered among them many of the Proprietors and merchants in Hudson. Names like Jenkins, Worth, Coffin, and Hathaway featured prominently in the Anti-Federalist camp. They met in the cozy back room of Judge Dayton's store, where they sat around a hot coal stove in a room blue with smoke and inveighed against what they thought was the intrusive and increasingly centralized authority of the new government and the influence upon it of aristocratic southern planters. The Federalists included many lawyers and professional men, and appealed to the younger and more progressive members of Hudson's population. They met more grandly in the best rooms of one of Hudson's better taverns. Both political parties maintained a marching band that turned out for parades and political rallies. The Anti-Federalists (or Republicans, as they were beginning to be known) wore a white uniform, while the Federalists (eventually the Democrats) wore red coats and white pantaloons.

Marching bands and marching soldiers became prominent features of Hudson life early on, creating organizations in which to fraternize, display civic pride, and perpetuate the patriotic spirit that had fueled the Revolutionary War. Even though the Revolution had ended, many felt that the old countries of Europe still posed a threat to the new republic. Moreover, Hudson, even at the end of the eighteenth century, was still close to a frontier. Across the river lay seemingly endless lands that were vast, dark, ancient, and threatening. Thick forests stretched toward the west. Hudsonians felt the need to raise protective forces to meet any possible threat—Indians, perhaps, or (as would later be the case) bands of disgruntled tenant farmers. Within a short time of its incorporation, Hudson's patriotic and civic-minded citizens raised a number of military companies. Captain Daniel Gano formed Hudson's first, called Gano's Artillery, in 1786. In 1788, Forthingham's Artillery marched in Hudson's first celebration of the Fourth of

July—a splendid affair featuring a salute of thirteen guns from Parade Hill. This was followed by an elegant dinner in Kellogg's Tavern for "the most respectable inhabitants of the city," and then "a most beautiful exhibition of fireworks" held for the pleasure of the entire citizenry, respectable or not.

Militias tried to outdo one another in the splendor of their uniforms. Captain Nicholas Hathaway's Infantry wore black cocked hats, blue coats faced with red, and white pantaloons. Captain Wigton's Artillery tried to outdo them with blue coats trimmed with red, blue pantaloons with red stripes, and black cocked hats with huge red plumes. The battle of the uniforms also reflected political bias. Some companies were made up of Federalists and others of Anti-Federalists, and they made no secret of their partisanship. The Federalist Hudson Greens, sporting green coats and pantaloons, black hats and green feathers, proudly marched in every Fourth of July celebration. Sometimes there were two or three celebrations sponsored by opposing parties, each one asserting that theirs was the most patriotic and most American.

Glorious though Hudson's many other military cadres were, and splendid as their uniforms could be, all were outdone by the Hudson Guards and the Scotch Plaids. The Hudson Guards were the pride of the city, so it is said, and marched in full ranks down Warren Street, glittering in their uniform of blue coat, bright silver buttons, white pantaloons, and a high, bucket-shaped leather hat from which floated a white feather plume almost half a yard long. Their friendly rivals were the Scotch Plaids, whose quirky outfit may have even outshone the Hudson Guards. The Plaids were said to be the favorite company of young Hudsonians. Their frock coats and pantaloons of bright plaid trimmed with black and gleaming buttons must have made a military fashion statement that no one soon forgot, not to mention their unique hat—an elegant black beaver with a huge cluster of black plumes falling down on either side.[20]

A woodcut showing characteristic American military uniforms of the early nineteenth century.

TWO

THIS STREET
IS NO LONGER MAIN STREET: 1790–1810

For the next twenty-five years or so, Hudson's trade and population continued to expand. By 1790 more than 2,500 people lived in Hudson, an increase of more than 1,000 in just five years. Hudson became a port of entry in 1790, and one into which goods from around the world were received. The Bank of Columbia was chartered in 1793, the third bank to be chartered in the state. As many as fifteen ships a day departed from Hudson carrying exports of beef, pork, shad herring, barrel staves, lumber, leather, and country produce. Most traded with other Hudson River ports, southern coastal ports, and the West Indies, although some were engaged in whaling and sealing. A Hudson whaler, the *American Hero,* returned to Hudson from the Pacific in 1797 carrying the largest cargo of sperm oil ever brought into the United States. In addition, Hudson had five or six vessels engaged in killing seals in the Falkland Islands and the South Atlantic. Oil, skins, and seal fur came back to Hudson. Skins were tanned into leather in Hudson's tanneries, located on what is now Tannery Lane. One was owned—not surprisingly—by a member of the Jenkins clan. Oil, both seal and whale, was turned into candles and lamp oil in the candle works of Thomas Jenkins on Diamond Street, between First and Second, and in Cotton Gelston's factory on the corner of Second and State Street.

All of this prosperity encouraged the Common Council to make their city more beautiful and to attempt to enhance the prestige of their main street. This was done by creating a park at the lower end near the river, changing the name of the street, and accepting land for a park at the upper end. The Proprietors voted in 1795 that "a certain piece of land known as the Parade, or Mall, in front of Main Street and on the bank fronting the river, should be granted to the common council forever, as public walk or mall, and for no other purpose whatever." This is Hudson's present-day Promenade Hill, then known as Parade Hill because Hudson's militia paraded there.

In 1799 Main Street ceased to exist. One day, Hudsonians saw messages in red and yellow chalked on fences along the street summarily informing them that "this street is no longer Main Street, but called Warren Street by order of the Common Council." It is a minor mystery as to why this was done so suddenly, and who the name change was meant to honor. No record can be found of any Hudson worthy named Warren. Several American towns, streets, taverns, and counties had been named in honor of General Joseph Warren, the Revolutionary War hero who fell at the Battle of Bunker Hill, and one possibility is that Hudson's Warren Street may also do him honor.

By 1800, buildings on Warren Street still did not extend much past Fourth Street, though a second market house was built near the prison on the north side of Warren at Fourth Street. Above that was still open country. The newly named Warren Street was a dirt track that led past the country house of Ezekiel Gilbert, which stood near or upon the site of the present St. Charles Hotel. In 1800, Gilbert donated to the city enough land from acreage surrounding his country house to create a public square. The square, which Gilbert intended for a city park, remained an empty lot for seventy-five years, though in a curious decision of the city fathers it was "for some inscrutable reason denuded of its fine old forest trees and paved with cobblestones."[21] Beyond the public square, Warren connected to another dirt road (later to be called Prospect Avenue), which led past the Hudson Academy to Claverack.

Hudson City, *watercolor by P. Lodet, circa 1806. Courtesy Franklin D. Roosevelt Library, Hyde Park. Gift of Mark Eisener to Franklin D. Roosevelt, 1933. This is the earliest known view of the city of Hudson.*

Because of the city's amazing economic and social growth in the late eighteenth century, Hudson's citizens were fueled by boundless confidence. How could they not be? The city's population dramatically increased again, going from 2,500 in 1790 to 4,000 in 1800. There was one ominous note, however. The last sealing vessel sailed in 1799, and with it went the brief period of whaling and sealing that had helped to buoy Hudson's economy during the last few years of the eighteenth century.

If there was unease about the future, no one expressed it. After all, an indubitable sign of progress came in 1807 in the form of Fulton's steamboat, which passed through Hudson's channel "without sails or oars, being propelled by a common water wheel, which was moved by the assistance of machinery with steam." Upon the steamboat's return downstream the next day, "every spot which afforded a sight of the river was crowded with people eager to get a view of the great curiosity."[22] With such wonders at hand, how could it not be believed that Hudson would continue to expand indefinitely? It probably occurred to no one that the clouds of steam pouring from the steamboat's tall funnel were the signal that the great days of sailing ships—upon which Hudson had made fortunes—were nearing the end.

Indeed, whaling and most of Hudson's sea trade had already been struck a mortal blow. During the French Revolution and the later Napoleonic wars, France and England levied embargoes against one another's ships. Consequently, merchants of both nations were willing to pay huge prices to ship their goods on neutral vessels. Many Hudson ship owners, unwisely as it turned out, abandoned their usual trade so as to take advantage of the high fees. They paid dearly for this. Britain and France decreed that any foreign ship trading with the enemy was subject to capture and confiscation. The American ships were no match for the huge British or French navies, and Hudson lost so many ships through seizure that its maritime trade was nearly destroyed. But the final blow to Hudson's sea trade came from America itself. In 1807, President Jefferson placed all ships within the jurisdiction of the United States under embargo to prevent their being used for trade with Europe. This embargo continued until 1830. Some of Hudson's ship owners defied the embargo, but the good times were over. Hudson lost not only a large part of its fleet, but its trading outlets as well.

THE END OF THE PROPRIETORS: 1810

In part because of this disaster, the rule of the Proprietors came to an end. In 1808, Thomas Jenkins died. He was *the* founding father, whose clan gave Hudson its mayors for thirty years. Its numbers reduced and its fortunes in decline, the association members voted to dissolve in 1810. They deeded what remained of the public lands of Hudson that they held as an association to the Common Council, and voted that their records should be delivered to the city.

The Proprietors had created Hudson and ruled it for three decades, both as a private association and later through mayors and the Common Council. They held Hudson very nearly as a private fiefdom. Most of Hudson's businesses belonged to them, and all of its land was vested in them, land which they sold off bit by bit and piece by piece only to those they felt could make a proper contribution to the city on a hill that they had built. Their vision was a practical one—to build a safe place to conduct the trade in which they all were already engaged. But it was also a breathtaking vision because it was courageous and imaginative. They found on the banks of the Hudson a frontier hamlet, and there they built a modern city and brought it prosperity and a burgeoning population. When the association dissolved, the city numbered nearly 200 houses and more than 4,000 people.

The last meeting of the Proprietors was apparently a contentious one, for old Cotton Gelston did not want to see the end of what he, as one of the original Proprietors, had helped begin. He refused to turn over the records of which he was custodian. Instead he tried to throw them into the fire, and did manage to burn some. But others of the august body restrained him, and on that acrimonious note on May 23, 1810, the Proprietors' Association came to an end.[23] The dissolution marked the end of "Old Hudson."

The Hudson waterfront circa 1820, showing the navigation channels cut for shipping into the so-called "middle ground." High above the river is the Parade, or what is now known as Parade Hill or the Promenade. Plate 4, No. 12, Amerique Septentrionale. Etat de New York, *by Jacques Louis Milbert. Collection of the Columbia County Historical Society, Kinderhook, New York.*

THE END OF SUMMER: 1830

The undignified and unhappy end of the Proprietors' Association seems in retrospect to be the signal that the city's fortunes were about to be eclipsed. Only four whaling ships left Hudson between 1808 and 1820.[24] The economic decline following the end of the War of 1812 further exacerbated the situation in Hudson. In 1815 Hudson lost its status as a port of entry. In 1819, after three years of currency inflation, financial panic led to the collapse of the national economy. The Bank of Hudson failed, taking with it the fortunes of many of Hudson's most prominent citizens. Soon, another blow to Hudson's eminence as a port was struck by the newly opened Erie Canal, which made it easy for products from the vast western lands to be shipped via the canal and the Hudson River directly to New York City. Many of those western products duplicated in much larger quantities what Hudson produced from its factories and outlying farms. Hudson had been bypassed, as Margaret Schram notes, by progress.[25]

Since there was little trade, few ships were needed and shipbuilding declined, as did the sail-making and rope-making industries connected with it. During the next twenty years only seventeen ships were built in Hudson. Of the great fleet that Hudson had once been able to put out to sea—huge ships of several hundred tons apiece carrying holds full of cargo to ports worldwide—now only a handful of small sloops remained, limited to desultory trade upon the river between Albany and New York City. Twenty years of hard times lay ahead for the city.

As if to put a seal upon misfortune, a devastating fire swept through lower Hudson in 1825. Beginning in Cherry Alley, the fire was fanned by a brisk wind, leaping from house to house and destroying many homes in the area of what is now First Street. It soon crossed Warren and continued its devastation as far as Diamond Street. It was finally checked through the efforts of the newly formed fire company.

With its warehouses empty and its factories idle, Hudson lost population for the first time since its founding. The 1820 census counted 5,300 inhabitants. By 1825 the population had decreased to less than 5,000. The grim mood of those who had thought that good fortune would never end resonated in a gloomy civic obituary written by William B. Stoddard in the *Rural Repository*: "The summer-like days of Hudson's commercial prosperity have passed, and public spirit and public pride are buried with no prospect of resurrection."[26]

HUDSON'S ARCHITECTURE: EARLY DUTCH, FEDERAL, AND GREEK REVIVAL STYLE, 1780s–1840s

Eighteenth-century America built its houses in the styles that its settlers brought from Europe, and Hudson was no different. The Dutch settlers in Columbia County and Hudson built in what has been called the "medieval tradition"—steep, gabled roofs, with massive beams and brick construction.[27] Only two early Dutch-style houses survive today in Hudson. The first, perhaps built when Hudson was Claverack Landing, is the Robert Taylor House. It is, in fact, an English house built in the late eighteenth century, but in the Dutch vernacular style. It is located on Tanner's Lane and was once on the banks of the South Bay. A photograph of the bay and the ironworks taken in the 1860s shows the house from the rear with its Dutch-style gambrel roof.

The other survivor is the Jan Van Hoesen House, located on the Dutch Acres Mobile Home Park on Route 66 in Claverack, just east of Claverack Creek. This was built between 1715 and 1724, and is one of seven similar brick dwellings to survive into the twenty-first century. On the east gable are the initials "T" and "JVH" worked into the masonry in black headers. These are the monograms of the first occupants of the house, Jan Van Hoesen (1687–1745) and his wife Tanneke, who married in 1711. Tanneke was a daughter of Hendrick Witbeck of Claverack. Jan was a grandson of Jan Frans Van Hoesen, who in 1662 purchased the tract of land from the Mohicans that the Proprietors would eventually buy and that now includes the city of Hudson and the town of Greenport.

When the Proprietors arrived, it is believed that some of them brought the frames of New England-style houses. But in a land of such plentiful timber, it is not likely that many felt obliged to come so prepared. They were familiar already, of course, with the dominant style of American architecture—Georgian—and the style known as Federal.

Georgian style developed in England during the late seventeenth and eighteenth centuries, and took its name from English kings George I, George II, and George III. Its design motifs were taken from Classical Roman, Italian Renaissance, and Palladian design—symmetry, formality, pedimented doors, and Palladian-style windows. Federal style, of which Thomas Jefferson was a leading exponent, was named for the newly formed federation of the United States. It turned away from the association with English monarchy that Georgian houses invoked, and looked instead to "democratic" ancient Greece and "republican" Rome for inspiration.

Many houses built in the 1780s, while emphasizing classical symmetry and motifs, employed designs made popular by Robert and James Adam in England, and thus adapted rather than rejected Georgian styles. They combined Georgian style with elements and motifs we now call Federal—fan lights, low relief ornamentation in the form of scrolls, medallions, and classical figures, arched windows surmounted with classical keystones, and doors framed by pilasters or classical columns. From the 1780s to the 1820s, several Georgian/Federal houses were built in Hudson.

The finest example of Federal architecture ever built in Hudson, and one of the greatest in America, was the circa 1790s Captain John Hathaway House, which once stood at 308 Warren Street. The Hathaway House was in the vernacular of great Federal-style buildings created by American architects Charles Bulfinch, Asher Benjamin, and Samuel McIntire, and was especially reminiscent of houses built by McIntire in Salem (with which the Proprietors were no doubt familiar).

Georgian/Federal architecture—whether in grand mansions or simpler, smaller homes—remained popular until about 1820. Thus, it was the dominant style during Hudson's building boom, and there are a larger number of buildings in this style than any other among the surviving structures of early Hudson.

Among other significant Hudson buildings in the Federal style that are still standing is the Seth Jenkins House (115 Warren Street, ca. 1795), a two-and-one-half-story, brick, Federal-style house with double marble steps, iron railings, and marble facing on the foundation. This house was built by Seth Jenkins, an original Proprietor, the city's first mayor, and brother of Thomas Jenkins, another of Hudson's original Proprietors whose house (ca. 1790s), in much altered condition, stands at 218–220 Warren. The

Robert Jenkins House (113 Warren Street, ca. 1811), is a two-and-one-half-story, brick, Federal-style house with five bays and delicate tracery in the Palladian window and door surrounds. It was built by Robert Jenkins, who was the son of Seth Jenkins and served as city mayor in 1808–1812 and 1815–1819. The Robert Jenkins House is now the headquarters of the Hendrick Hudson Chapter of the National Society of the Daughters of the American Revolution, having been given to them by Jenkins's granddaughter.

Another notable survivor from this period is the former Bank of Hudson (116 Warren Street, ca. 1809), which contains both Federal and Greek Revival features, including an ornamental marble frieze, marble pilasters, and medallions, built by John C. Hogeboom, probably a descendent of Peter Hogeboom, one of the early Dutch settlers of Claverack Landing. In nearby

View of Hudson from Athens, circa 1820. Engraving by Hill after a watercolor by William Guy Wall, Hudson River Portfolio *(1820-1826). Collection of the Columbia County Historical Society, Kinderhook, New York.*

Greenport—then still part of Hudson—are two other noteworthy examples of the Federal style: the traditionally Federal Alexander Jenkins House (Joslyn Boulevard, ca. 1818), and the unusual and innovative Joab Center House (ca. 1812–1821), which was once situated in the midst of a large sheep farm.

One of Hudson's greatest houses, built as the Hudson Almshouse, is now the Hudson Area Association Library on State Street. This Federal stone structure was built in 1818 by Ephraim Baldwin, under the supervision of a building committee made up of Hudson residents Dr. John Talman, Judah Paddock, and Barnabus Waterman. It was based on plans drawn by Robert Jenkins, twice mayor of the city and nephew of the most eminent of the city's founders, Thomas Jenkins. The building is unique in Hudson not only because of its stone (rather than brick) materials, but because it is an unusual and excellent example of Federal institutional style. As such, it is one of Hudson's three or four most important early landmarks, ranking in historical and architectural significance with the Worth House (ca. 1795) on Union Street, the Seth Jenkins House (ca. 1795) at 115 Warren Street, the Samuel Plumb House (1811), and the 1811 house of Robert Jenkins (the almshouse's designer) at 113 Warren, to which it is significantly related stylistically.

The almshouse was built for the city's poor, and the location was carefully chosen so as to make it the focal point of the Fourth Street corridor that traverses the city from State Street to

The city of Hudson circa 1824. Engraving for the Rural Repository. *Collection of Margaret B. Schram.*

Washington Square Park, the site of another one of Hudson's most architecturally important buildings—the present Warren and Wetmore-designed courthouse.

In 1830 the almshouse became the Hudson Asylum for the Insane, founded by Hudson resident Dr. Samuel White, who pioneered the humane care and treatment of mental patients in the asylum. In 1851 the asylum closed and the building became the Hudson Female Academy. Among those who taught at the academy was artist Henry Ary, a Hudson resident and one of the early painters of the Hudson River School. Ary's paintings of Mt. Merino, the South Bay, the Hudson River, and the city of Hudson are touchstones of those subjects. His portrait of George Washington can be seen in today's Hudson City Hall.

The academy closed in 1865, and from then until 1881 the building was the residence of George Power. Power was a major force in the development of Hudson ferries and other river transportation. Born in 1817, Power was a seaman and eventually became the owner of the New York and Hudson Steamboat Company, the Hudson and Athens Ferry, and the Hudson and Catskill Ferry. The ferryboat that ran between Hudson and Athens bore his name. Power was one of the original trustees of the Hudson City Savings Institution (now the Hudson River Bank and Trust) and served two terms as the mayor of Hudson. Much of the grander interior detail of the modern-day library, such as the marble fireplaces and the marble entry hall, dates from Power's ownership of the building.

In 1881 the building returned to the service of the people of Hudson as the new home of the Hudson Orphan Asylum, which had been founded by Sally McKinstry. McKinstry was born in Hudson in 1798 and remained actively involved with the orphanage until her death in 1862. The orphanage remained at this State Street site until 1957.

Ownership of the building then passed to the Children's Foundation, which donated the property to the Hudson City School District in 1959 with the stipulation that the building become a library for the people of the city of Hudson. The school district has owned the building for half a century, during which time it has been the home of the Hudson Area Association Library.

Another important Hudson house that also survived, even though abandoned in the 1970s, is the Samuel Plumb House (now the Plumb–Bronson House) on Worth Avenue on the grounds of the Hudson Correctional Facility. This Federal house was subject to several renovations over the years after its construction in 1811, very likely by Barnabus Waterman, the master builder to whom the Vander Poel House in Kinderhook is attributed. William Guy Wall provided an early picture of the house, one of the earliest known images of any Hudson house, in an 1819 watercolor. This landscape, painted from a vantage point probably near the present reservoir, shows Mt. Merino and the South Bay. In the center, as the focal point, is the house built for Samuel Plumb, a New Englander who followed the original Proprietors to Hudson.

In 1838 the house of Samuel Plumb was purchased by Dr. Oliver Bronson. Bronson's father had been a major figure in New York City banking, and Oliver Bronson was a man of considerable wealth. The year after he bought the house, Bronson hired Alexander Jackson Davis to refit it in the picturesque style that was gaining great popularity in the country at that time. Davis extended the roof to create projecting eaves, and added ornamental brackets. He also added a veranda with ornamental fretwork to the east façade of the house, which is significant because it was one of earliest ornamental verandas in the United States. These 1839 alterations are of particular importance because they are very early examples of the uniquely American style of architecture that has come to be known as Hudson River Bracketed, a style for which Davis is the acknowledged inventor.

In 1849, Davis was again commissioned by Bronson, this time to expand his house in the new Italianate style. Davis added the west façade that overlooks the South Bay and the river, a deep veranda with ornamental fretwork, an octagonal center vestibule, matching semi-octagonal parlors, and a three-story tower. In his alterations to the house, Davis respected many of the details of the original Federal design, including the magnificent elliptical staircase, and seamlessly integrated them into his new conception.

Now a National Historic Landmark, the Plumb–Bronson House will undergo a lengthy process of stabilization and restoration under the stewardship of the all-volunteer preservation group, Historic Hudson.

In the 1820s, Greek Revival replaced Federal as the dominant style of American architecture. Greek Revival, as its name implies, derived elements from classical Greece, including the use of columned porticoes, pilasters, and other motifs. As the nation expanded, the style moved westward. Greek Revival had as an advantage that simple, private homes—as well as grand mansions and great public buildings—could employ its classic, pedimented, temple design. In Hudson, some Federal houses were modernized to Greek Revival in the 1830s, and the style remained fashionable until about 1860.

One of the best surviving examples of the style in Hudson is the Curtiss House, built about 1834 by Cyrus Curtiss, an agent for a whaling company and the mayor of Hudson in 1844. The house is in what might be called urban Greek Revival style with Ionic columns. The octagonal cupola on the roof, known as a "widow's walk," provides a good view of the Hudson River. Two other intact examples of the style, with columned porticos and classic temple facades, are 738 Warren Street and St. Michael's Church on Partition Street below Second Street. At the corner of City Hall Place and Warren Street is the Hudson Opera House, formerly city hall, built in 1855 in the Greek Revival style. It was used as the city hall for over one hundred years until 1962.

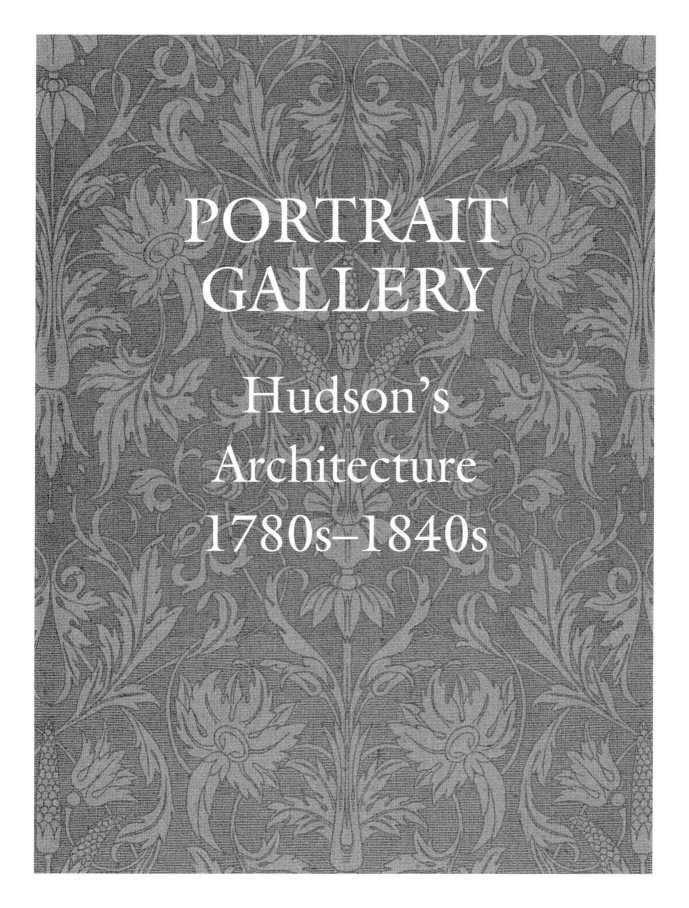

PORTRAIT GALLERY

Hudson's Architecture 1780s–1840s

The late-eighteenth-century, gambrel-roofed Robert Taylor House, seen from the rear at the right of the picture, circa 1860s. This early Hudson house is located at the end of Cross Street and once looked over the South Bay.

The Captain John Hathaway House in a photograph from the 1860s. One of the finest Federal houses in the nation, it was built in the late eighteenth century and was located on Warren above Third Street. Later, as shown here, it was embellished with Greek Revival ornamentation.

This late-eighteenth-century, brick, Georgian-style building was located on lower Warren Street and housed the Hudson River Bank. It was updated in the early nineteenth century in a simple Greek Revival style.

A late-eighteenth-century, Georgian-style, brick building, updated in the early nineteenth century in a more ornate Greek Revival style, located at 244 Warren Street. Note the Federal roof balustrade and the Greek Revival portico, both now missing.

This Federal brick house with five bays and typical fan-light above the door, located at 113 Warren Street, was built in 1811 by Robert Jenkins—twice mayor of Hudson, and brother of Seth Jenkins. The Robert Jenkins House is the home of the DAR and is a museum of the city of Hudson.

This Federal brick building located at 116 Warren Street housed the former Bank of Hudson. The building was probably designed by Barnabas Waterman about 1809 for John C. Hogeboom, who was most likely a descendent of Peter Hogeboom, one of the original Dutch settlers of Claverack Landing. The house contains both Federal and Greek Revival features, including marble pilasters and medallions. The original center entrance was moved to the side about 1820 when the Greek Revival portico was added.

This Federal stone structure was built in 1818 by Ephraim Baldwin (based on plans drawn by Robert Jenkins) as the Hudson Almshouse. In 1830 the almshouse became the Hudson Asylum for the Insane. In 1851 the Hudson Female Academy occupied the building, and after the academy closed it became the residence of George Power from 1865 to 1881. In 1881 it housed the Hudson Orphan Asylum, which remained there until 1957. In 1959 the Hudson Area Association Library was given the use of the building when it was acquired by the Hudson City School District through a gift from the Children's Foundation, then owners of the property. Collection of the Columbia County Historical Society, Kinderhook, New York.

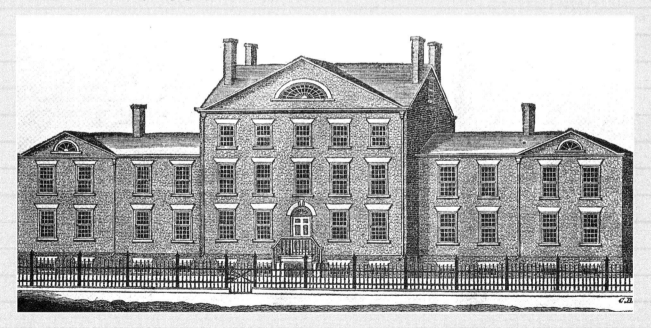

This classic Greek Revival house is located at 738 Warren Street. Collection of Hank and Debbie DiCintio.

Greek Revival house located on Partition Street. It is now St. Michael's Orthodox Church.

THREE

HUDSON WILL AGAIN FLOURISH AS IN ITS INFANT DAYS: 1830–1845

In an attempt to reverse the dire situation into which the city had fallen, a group of citizens decided to take to the sea again in 1829. A new association was formed, the Hudson Whaling Company, composed not of confident old Proprietors but of men who may have been desperate and who may have gambled all they had in an attempt to revive the glory days of Hudson's whaling industry. How much hope was invested in the project and how desperately it was needed may be read between the lines of the plaintive query of a contemporary account: "Why may we not hope to rival those eastern cities which the whale fishery has built up? We possess equal advantages, equal enterprise." The Hudson Whaling Company launched its first ship, the *Alexander Mansfield,* in June 1830. The voyage began in the hope that upon its safe return, "Hudson will again flourish as in its infant days."

That hope was realized. After nine long months during which there was no word from the ship, the *Alexander Mansfield* was sighted coming upriver on Sunday, March 27, 1831. Crowds poured into the streets and down to the riverfront. Cannons were fired and church bells were rung. Imagine the excitement and tense anticipation that must have been felt by those who had risked all in this venture. How long it must have seemed to the anxious crowd on the shore for the square-rigged ship to make its way to the dock. When the ship finally docked and was secured, Captain Bennett came down the gangplank to deliver his news to the waiting owners, announcing that the *Alexander Mansfield* carried in its hold more than 2,000 barrels of whale oil, 100 barrels of sperm oil, and 14,000 pounds of whalebone. The "acclamations of the citizens and sailors" exploded into near frenzy, for that huge cargo was among the largest that any ship had yet brought into the United States.

With that success behind it, the *Alexander Mansfield* sailed again within two months to the south Atlantic, this time commanded by Francis Neil—its former first mate—and with a crew of thirty young men from Hudson. Captain Bennett was given the newer and larger *Meteor*. Both ships returned within a few months' time, each laden with thousands of barrels of oil and thousands of pounds of whalebone. Later that year, the America docked and the amazing news soon spread all over town that the ship carried an astounding cargo of oil valued at more than $80,000—the equivalent of more than $1.5 million today.

Hudson seemed to have been reborn. Hudson's whalers were once again sailing the seas. In 1832, Hudson had eight ships at sea. In 1833 it had ten. Once again the engine of progress appeared to be unstoppable. Banks were chartered. Houses were built. New people came to the city and its population climbed again. Hudson expanded uptown. But despite the expansion, it was at this time that the Common Council voted—in what now seems an odd and shortsighted decision—to cede more than three-quarters of the original area incorporated in 1785 to the town of Stockport in 1833 and to the town of Greenport in 1837, thus reducing the city to an enclave of two-and-one-half square miles surrounded on three sides by the huge town of Greenport, and on the fourth by the river.

Now that there was money again, some Hudsonians began to ask if the face of the city might not be improved. The gloomy writer who lamented the end of Hudson's prosperous summer was one of those who hoped that Hudson had the means and the will to make improvements. "Our object now," he said, "is, while our citizens are looking about them for objects of improvement, and are not only able, but willing to expend their means in the public good, humbly to suggest a channel where their efforts might be most usefully directed. We mean, the improvement of our public buildings." Hudson's public buildings were its government buildings, its schools, and its churches. The courthouse stood on the corner of Warren and Fourth Street, the jail was across the street, and the Asylum for the Insane (in the 1818 building now occupied by the Hudson Area Association Library) stood on State Street. Hudson's academies were all private schools. These consisted of the Lancaster Society (furnishing classes to the poor) at Fourth and State Street, the Hudson Academy on Academy Hill, and the Hudson Select Academy at Allen and Third Street. In 1830, Hudson had six churches: the Quaker meetinghouse, the Presbyterian, Methodist, and Episcopal churches; the Baptist church at the corner of Fourth and State Street; and the Universalist church at the corner of Third and Allen Street. Few of these buildings pleased the writer, who complained that "with the exception of the lunatic asylum there is not a single edifice among them which is honorable to the city." His inventory proceeded:

Let us take for instance the Court House, occupying a prominent position in Warren street. ... While we realize what such a building should be, we blush when we see what it is. A large, unsymmetrical, decaying pile, from the exterior surface of which the paint has been obliterated long since, the ceilings of which are cracking, and the timbers trembling like the limbs of an ague patient, or the shrunk bones of Ezekiel's valley. Will the Board of Supervisors permit such a structure to stand? If something is not done speedily, the trouble of demolishing it will be saved; it will come down of its own accord; the very swallows whose countless tribes have tenanted its belfry for years, are forsaking it. We must likewise enter our remonstrance against the location of a gaol in front of our principal thoroughfare, and suggest a speedy removal. Our churches are also in a miserable condition. Every strong wind shakes their steeples, and enters within doors most unceremoniously. There is nothing of architectural finish, or even comfort about them. The same remarks may be applied to our Academies. Fellow citizens, shall these things be? It has been said that "the public buildings of a city are its ornament or disgrace." Let us weigh well the truth of this remark, and be up and doing.[28]

As if to answer these objections, Hudson did begin to build. A new county courthouse was certainly needed; the old one at Fourth Street was small and outdated. In 1833 the Common Council acquired a large plot of land at the end of Fourth Street bounded by Union Street. There, in 1835, the first courthouse on what would be called Washington Square was built. It was a simple and elegant Greek Revival building with a dome and six Ionic columns. The building stood for the rest of the century, and then it too was deemed too small and was torn down. The old courthouse on the corner of Warren and Fourth Street had been demolished in 1835 and the land sold to the Presbyterians, who felt the need for more space than their church on Federal Street (Allen Street) allowed. They sold that church and it was demolished a few years later. The Presbyterians returned to their first site of worship and there built a new, Gothic-style church to which they affixed their weathervane. The old jail, which had been erected in 1805 on the corner of Warren and Fourth Street, was purchased and remodeled by John Davis. Known as Davis Hall, the building housed city hall.

The riverfront Parade Hill, which had been given to the city in 1795, underwent beautification in the early 1830s. For some years the park had been called Round House Hill because of the existence there of an octagonal building that had been used as a lookout post from which a flag was raised or a horn was blown to announce the arrival of an approaching ship. The Round House (or Flag House, as it was usually called) boasted a room for refreshments on the lower floor and a covered porch or piazza on the upper story for viewing the Catskills. The Flag House became a place to consort with neighbors. There, under the direction of Cornelius Myers, one could be served "the choicest delicacies, both eatable and drinkable" and "those rarities which Hudson cannot furnish," including "Oranges, Pine Apples, Lemons, Figs, Raisins, Prunes, Grapes, Nuts of various kinds, Ice-creams, and the best of liquors and whatever may be necessary to enhance their relish." Myers offered "a pleasant apartment on the first floor fitted up with seats and tables furnished with newspapers where the news can be read and public events talked about, with as much summer comfort as any room on the continent." As if this were not enough, the second floor provided a "charming prospect" that was "unrivalled by an inland view in America or any where else." To this exclusive domain "none but subscribers will be admitted," and for them "a spy-glass will be kept to assist the eye." Myers assured Hudson that the establishment would be "frequented by none but decent company" and nothing would take place there that was "incompatible with public decorum."[29]

Oddly, this structure was demolished in 1835, the same year that the park was officially named Parade Hill. Some had hoped that it would be called Paradise Hill. This hope may have stemmed from the fact that the site apparently possessed a circular grove of trees called the "Lovers Retreat." Inside this grove, it was said, was a large stone outcropping called "Love Rock." There "by moonlight alone," so Stephen B. Miller claims, "a large proportion of the marriage contracts of our Quaker ancestors were made." In 1834 the rock was leveled. A writer in a Hudson paper at the time hints at scenes of Quaker abandon taking place around Hudson's Love Rock late on moonlit nights: "Men among us whose heads are white with the snow-flakes of time have sat upon it with the buoyant passions of youth. Women who can scarce raise their feeble limbs have leaped in glorious glee around its base. How many bright moons have shed their light upon it; how many strains of music floated away in the air above it … We have sat there ourselves and might tell curious things about it."[30]

In 1837 a new hotel was built—the Worth Hotel (then called Hudson House), on Warren between First and Second streets across from the house built by Thomas Jenkins. This soon came to be known as Hudson's best hotel and became the lodging of choice for travelers to Hudson in the nineteenth century. Its one hundred rooms were deemed luxurious by any standard.

The year 1837 also saw the establishment of one of Hudson's more enduring cultural institutions—the Franklin Library Association. Occupying a room on Union Street near the present site of Christ Church, the library began to amass a collection that numbered more than 5,000 volumes by the end of the century. The library soon became a place for cultural pursuits and socializing, and joined Hudson's other "improvement societies"—like the Columbia Moral Society (1815), the Hudson Forum (1826), and the Hudson Association for Mutual Improvement (1834). The anti-slavery movement appeared in Hudson in the 1830s as sentiment against slavery slowly increased. A meeting of the Anti-Slavery Society held in the Baptist Church in 1838 was addressed by speakers from the society and chaired by Alexander Coffin, the last of the Proprietors. Sentiment may have been strong within the society, but when it came to the ballot box, the anti-slavery candidate lost by a huge margin.

Amid these positive developments, however, came a crippling blow. The depression of 1837 was about to devastate the nation, taking Hudson with it and leaving the city to limp along as its attempt at revival briefly glowed, then dimmed, and slowly died. This was the worst depression in American history up to that time, causing financial ruin and misery to millions. Hundreds of banks and businesses failed, and thousands of people lost their land.

The number of Hudson ships leaving port began an irreversible decline, which may have been barely noticed amid the general collapse. In 1838, Hudson had nine ships at sea. In 1840 there were only five. By 1844 only two remained, and the last whaling voyage ended in 1845. Whaling was no longer profitable. The discovery of camphene, a turpentine distillation used for lighting, helped decrease the demand for sperm whale oil. Hudson's last whaler, the *Martha* (the name means "she who becomes bitter"), was sold at auction and "from that time Hudson knew no more of harpoons and lances" and never again saw "a square rigger at her wharves."[31]

In later years, as memories dimmed, many Hudsonians liked to imagine that early Hudson was primarily a whaling town and that whaling was the industry upon which its prosperity was founded. Whaling indeed played a part in Hudson's early history, but that part should not be exaggerated. Only a few of Hudson's ships were actually engaged in whaling, and that venture lasted only for a few years, roughly from 1785 until the War of 1812. Whaling helped Hudson prosper in the eighteenth century, and it did help bring back some prosperity for a time in the nineteenth century, but it was never Hudson's primary source of income. As compared with other American whaling ports, Hudson rated only eighteenth in the number of whaling vessels put to sea, and twenty-fourth in the number of voyages made. Margaret B. Schram provides a definitive discussion of this subject in *Hudson's Merchants and Whalers: The Rise and Fall of a River Port, 1783–1850*. In judging Hudson's final whaling venture in the 1830s and 1840s, Schram observes: "Hudson's whale fishery died because the idea was flawed to begin with. In trying to revive the glory days of the 1700s, Hudson only managed to financially distress its citizens."[32]

Hudson's troubles were exacerbated by two terrible fires in 1838 and 1844. The fire of 1838 was one of the most destructive ever in Hudson. The fire began, it was said, from a spark from the steamboat *Congress*, which was docked at the waterfront. A strong wind carried the fire to the warehouse of Samuel Plumb. The conflagration then quickly

The Fire of 1838, by William H. Clark. Collection of FASNY Museum of Firefighting, Hudson, New York.

spread until the entire area bounded by Second and Partition streets, the South Bay, and Water Street was engulfed. The fire destroyed warehouses and more than seventy residences including the gabled, Dutch, John Van Alen House. At least one hundred families were made homeless. The burned and vacant ground was eventually laid out as Franklin Square. In 1844 the area around the new square was again visited by fire. Sparks from a steamboat were the cause once again. Three wharves, several warehouses, and about thirty other buildings were burned. The damage caused by the fires is estimated to have been more than $8 million in today's money. Lost in the flames were the earliest buildings of old Hudson and whatever may have survived from the even older Claverack Landing. If one believed in omens, this wholesale destruction did not bode well.

The sinking of the Steamboat Swallow, *artist unknown, 1845. Collection of Historic Hudson.*

Wreck of the **STEAM BOAT SWALLOW** *on the night of April 1845 near Hudson having on board between 3 to 4 hundred passengers most of w rescued by the Steam Boat Express, many valuable lives were lost.*

Historic Hudson ❀ An Architectural Portrait

And there was more to come. In 1842 and again in 1848, Hudson was visited by an equally destructive calamity—the Asian cholera. The Common Council closed the port in 1842 because of the cholera, and in the summer of 1848 the city itself "was shut up like Sunday," as one contemporary source said.[33]

Then there was the terrible accident of the night of April 7, 1845. The city was awakened by the frantic ringing of bells. People ran to Parade Hill, where a terrible sight met their eyes. The great steamboat *Swallow,* having hit a rock in the river channel, was broken in two, in flames, and sinking. The pitiful cries of the drowning could be heard distinctly from the hill, and though boats were sent to the rescue and some passengers were saved, more than forty drowned.

The wreck of the *Swallow* may have seemed a fitting symbol for the wreck of Hudson itself. With its once-great port gone quiet, Hudson entered into a nearly fatal period of decline. The "end of ocean navigation" was also the end forever "of the old order of things in Hudson."[34]

A Melancholy Air to Every Thing around It: Hudson at Mid-Century

Hudson's streets were no longer filled with merchants and sailors home from the sea. Its warehouses were no longer packed with barrels of whale oil and seal skins, as they had been in the eighteenth and early nineteenth century. Because shipbuilding had ceased, the ropewalk was silent, the shipyards were closed, and sailmakers made no more sails. Some believed that Hudson was "finished." One of those who thought so was Ignatius Jones. In *Recollections of Hudson,* written in 1847, Jones takes a gloomy view that may have summed up the general malaise:

> The days of its prosperity have long since passed away. Its population has decreased, its wealth diminished, its business sources have dried up, and almost every vestige of its former glory has disappeared. There are now no shipping at its docks, and no ships building. There is now no ring of the anvil to be heard,— no sound of the axe or the hammer. There is no bustle of seamen along its wharves, no song of the rope-maker upon its hills, no throng of wagons from the interior, no crowds of men in its streets. The shipyards are overgrown with grass, the wharves have moldered away, the ropewalk is deserted, the warehouses are empty, and the once busy crowds have long since disappeared. It is only on the arrival or departure of a steamboat that any decided signs of life are visible. The silent, and half-depopulated town seems to communicate a melancholy air to every thing around it.[35]

But this dire picture of Hudson in 1847 is somewhat at odds with another contemporary source. A sense of what Hudson life must have been like at the time can be surmised from the December 16, 1847, issue of the *Columbia Washingtonian,* "A Family Newspaper Devoted to Temperance, Morality, Education, Agriculture and General Intelligence," published in Hudson by A. N. Webb. The paper carried a foreign news column, some fiction, essays intended to improve, stock market reports, meeting announcements, and many columns of advertisements for local businesses. Looking at its yellowed pages now offers a snapshot of a vanished and not entirely "finished" Hudson, although there may be found hints that all is not well between the lines of the merchants' advertisements that offer better prices for cash.

A WALK ON WARREN IN 1847

Although whalers no longer docked at Hudson's wharves, steamships did. The first steamboat from the city was the *Bolivar,* launched in 1825 and captained by John Power. Soon, several ships were passing regularly between New York City and Hudson carrying freight and passengers upriver and downriver: the *Legislator,* the *Rockland,* and Captain John T. Haviland's *General Jackson.* The first steamships, like Fulton's were small, but soon much larger ships were built. Some were huge, many-decked affairs with tall stacks. The *Redfield* and the *Nuhpa* were especially grand. In the 1840s and 1850s, ships with locally evocative names like the *Columbia,* the *Knickerbocker,* and the *Berkshire* docked at Hudson, as did the *City of Hudson,* which ran the

The Arcade at Seventh Street and Warren Street. Collection of Jeremiah Rusconi.

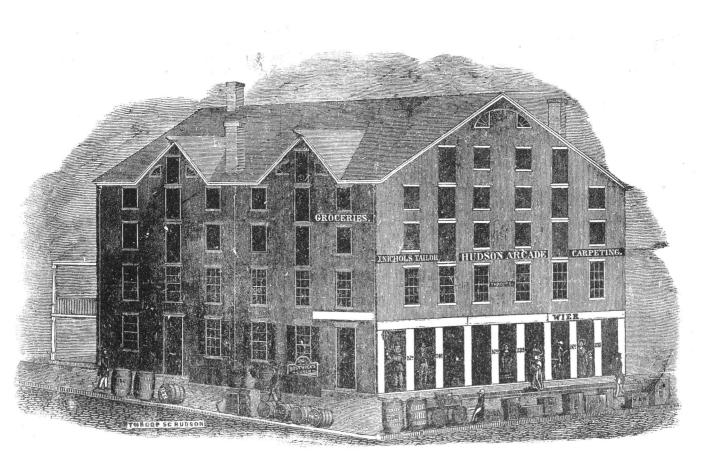

Shopping at Cyrus Macy's shop at 133 (now 305) Warren Street.

Hudson's dandies lounge in front of Tilley and Aldcroft, clothiers, located on the corner of Warren and South Fourth streets.

Historic Hudson ❀ An Architectural Portrait

Catskill–Albany line. How different it all must have seemed to the few like Captain Coffin (the last of the Proprietors, who died in 1840) who could still recall the day fifty or so years earlier when the *Joseph* docked, carrying Hudson's first Proprietor families, or when the fast little vessel *Freelove* brought necessaries and little luxuries from New York City to Hudson.

We learn from advertisements in the 1847 *Columbia Washingtonian* that anyone wishing to go from Hudson to New York City could do so every day, catching the 6:00 PM departure of the steamboat *Hudson* on Tuesdays, Thursdays, or Sundays, or that of the *Fairfield* on Mondays, Wednesdays, or Fridays. Both ships returned from New York City on the alternate days, and both made connections with the "cars from the east"—that is, with the trains coming from Berkshire County, Massachusetts. Rail travel was a chancy affair in 1847, and there were few comforts. Cars were almost without springs, and the track was narrow and uneven.

A visitor arriving from New York City had a choice of places to stay. There was the new National Hotel on Franklin Square, which was "conducted on temperance principles" and boasted "large and airy rooms built expressly for convenience and comfort." The owner, D. B. Stranahan, promised that "no exertions shall be wanted on his part to give perfect satisfaction to all who may patronize him." Amenities included "good stabling" and "carriages in attendance at the railroad depot to take passengers to the House free of charge." Or the choice might be the grand Worth Hotel (then still known as Hudson House), located on Warren Street just above Second Street and boasting equally comfortable rooms and a good restaurant.

If the visitor chose the Hudson House, a carriage would take him there. As he rode he might marvel at the changes in Hudson from the time he was here last, just a few years ago. The dock area, so recently devastated by a huge fire, was almost completely rebuilt. The new Franklin Square bustled with activity. As he was driven up Warren, he would see that in the last few years every lot had been purchased and built upon. Arriving at Hudson House, elegant in the new Greek Revival style that had been all the rage for a few years, he would find that his room was modern and large as promised, and that the restaurant was excellent indeed and revealed no threat of temperance principles. After a good dinner and a good night's sleep, he would be ready on the next day for his business rendezvous.

Shops lined Warren Street all the way from the river almost up to the public square at Seventh Street. Temptation met the eye at every turn. Almost every shop asserted that its wares would not be hard on the purse, many claiming in their advertisements that what they sold was cheaper at their emporiums than in any other place in the city, or the state, or indeed the world. They might be even cheaper for "CASH," as they often emphatically declared in their ads. A Hudson lady looking for fine pastries for the tea table, or perhaps for a tea table itself and all its accoutrements, or a fine new hat, or a simple piece of jewelry, could find it all in Hudson.

One could visit William Armstrong, whose store was at 283 Warren, just opposite the offices of the *Washingtonian*. At Armstrong's could be found "cloths, cashmeres, vestings, stocks, collars, bosoms, shoes and gloves" in "the most fashionable style and at prices to suit the times."

From there it was but a step to visit the new "Fancy Store" opened by Mrs. Haws, who announced in the paper that she was selling ladies' "dress caps, or other kinds of

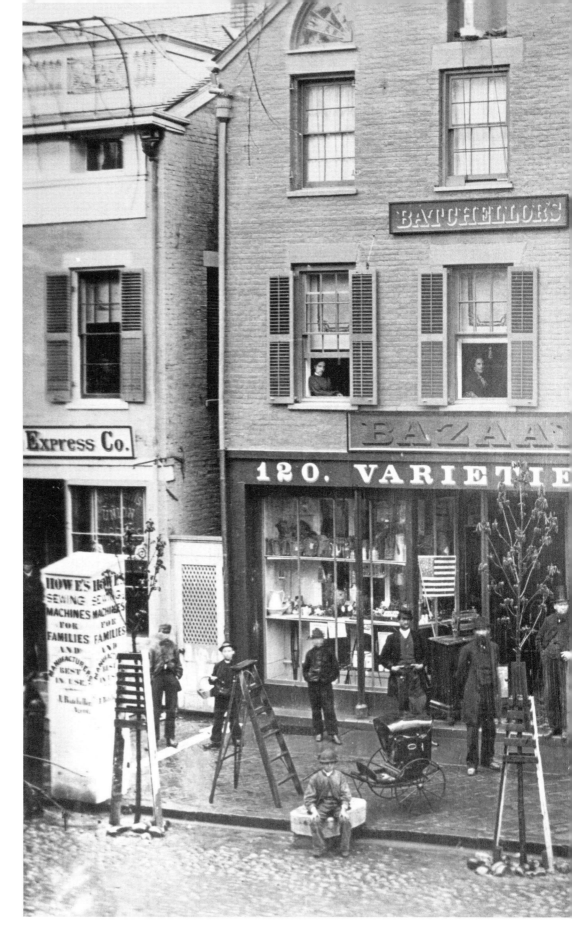

Batchellor's Variety store (circa 1860s) was located on the north side of Warren below Third Street.

lace," as well as ribbons, thread, and needles. Perhaps a pause at Mr. Rockefeller's at 329 Warren Street would also be in order. Rockefeller not only sold everything that Mr. Armstrong offered, but advertised, in addition, a fine stock of "French and English clothes." Or the choice might be J. P. Nichols, whose store was on upper Warren opposite Hannah's Jewelry. Mr. Nichols's announced that the "spring and summer fashions from New York have just been received." Who could resist that? And if a hat was needed, then a visit to Robert Tompkins would be so simple since his store "just opposite J. I. Gaul store at the head of the street" not only sold "muffs, buffalo robes, and fur collars," but also hats and caps. An added inducement was that Mr. Tompkins had "just returned from New-York with a splendid selection" of hats. Rounding out the list was the always intriguing Hudson Arcade at Seventh Street.

It was a pity that poor Peter Decker, "having disposed of his Boot and Shoe establishment and being desirous of having those indebted to him to call immediately" to settle their accounts, was no longer in the business of making shoes. But if shoes were needed, one could visit Allen Reynolds's new leather store on the west side of the public square at Seventh Street and peruse his collection of "sole and upper leather," though to get shoes made one might have to go to Clark and Mercer in distant Valatie. They advertised that they "pay particular attention to the manufacture of boots and shoes." If paint, window blinds, or a lamp chimney were needed, there was Tobey's, at the "sign of the whales jaw" at 229 Warren Street.

There was so much to see and do. Indeed, one might want to turn one's attention to beauty. Would it be daring to buy the "new invention for curling hair" called "Roby's Brazilian Hair Curler Liquid," as advertised by Punderson and Ham? One application, it was claimed, of this "delightful perfumed fluid will make the hair curl beautifully, resembling nature in Her greatest perfection. It is entirely free from grease." What if it did not work? What would be the result: straight and lanky hair, or no hair at all? If the latter, one could always apply "The Magic Fluid" sold at Rossman and McKinstry, which was "acknowledged by those who use it daily to be the best remedy to prevent baldness."

To change one's appearance and provide curls where there were none before, or simply to provide hair itself, one could purchase "wigs, toupees, frisettes or fronts" from William Green, whose store lay just below the William Badegely Mansion House, two doors down from Skinner's Dry Goods. Mr. Green sold his hair pieces at prices "cheaper than can be purchased in this city or any other" and could supply as well "braids for the head in all sizes and colors." S. F. Crossman also offered "all kinds of plain and curled hair work" as well as "wigs and scalps" (by which he meant "all kinds of gentleman's hair work"), and all "very cheap, for CASH." Indeed, hair seemed not only to be for sale, but eminently salable; Williams advertised "advanced prices for long hair."

To finish the "look," a trinket, bauble, necklace, or brooch might have seemed necessary. Both Hannah's and Wheeler's jewelry stores, prodigally competitive (each took out numerous three-line ads in the paper), advertised watches, gold lockets and miniature fob chains, "card cases, arrows, stelletoes," cameo and coral bracelets, and all manner of combs including shell side combs, finely carved back combs, dressing combs, long combs, twist combs, and horn combs—all meant to groom or decorate hair, whether one's own or discreetly purchased on Warren Street.

A display in the window of Rossman and McKinstry Pharmacists at 325 Warren Street might have attracted the eye, for they seemed to offer remedies for every complaint. One could not be too careful of one's health in those days, for as the tempting little boxes of Rev. B. Hibbard's Vegetable Pills warned, disease "comes upon us like a thief in the night." But armed with these pills, which were "the very best family medicine extant" and capable of "saving life as well as being a sovereign purifier of the blood," one would be protected from "general inflammatory diseases of the glands," not to mention all "derangements of the stomach." They also claimed to give "tone and energy to the whole system."

Then there was Dr. Le Rees's more exotic Persian Female Vegetable Pills, without doubt the most "perfect safe and efficacious" medicine ever provided to a "suffering humanity" for the "cure of female complaints." How, a mid-nineteenth-century shopper might have wondered, could they so plainly and openly advertise such things? Then, right there in plain sight was an actual Thompson Premium Truss, boldly, indeed almost lasciviously displayed.

Oriental-looking boxes of Roadway's Chinese Medicated Soap and Hunt's Liniment would catch the eye as well. The first promised to cure "chipped, cracked and repulsive skin"; the other, when massaged into the painful area, promised to end "rheumatism, complaints of the nervous system, sore throat and weak joints." Would it be idle to wonder if rheumatic pains in wrists and ankles might really be aided by Christie's Galvanic Rings or by Christie's Magnetic Fluid? The former claimed to harness the "mysterious power of galvanism" when worn "as an infallible agent to cure gout, tic, doloreux, toothache, vertigo, indigestion, paralysis, dizziness." They were said to be especially efficacious when worn after taking a healthy dose of the Magnetic Fluid—a lovely liquid whose effects reputably were pleasurable in the extreme, calming the nerves and giving a sense of instant well-being even as the mysterious power of magnetism, operating through the agency of Mr. Christie's various rings, bracelets, and bands ("made of all sizes and of various ornamental patterns" that "can be worn by the most delicate female without inconvenience") did their work. Or perhaps a good dose of Townsend's Sarsaparilla would do the trick—so delicious, so oddly satisfying. Indeed, one probably had friends that depended on it, resorting to its curative properties several times a day.

A stop at Hannah's Jewelry was absolutely imperative, for in addition to lovely things to wear, all manner of home furnishings were on display. For the table there were ivory napkin rings, fine cutlery, and Britannia ware—a lovely pewter set that included coffee urns and teapots, sugar bowls and creamers, cake baskets, pitchers, molasses cups, and candlesticks. Hannah's carried ivory goods, also: teething rings, whistles, chessmen, thimble cases, snuffboxes, and crochet needles. There were even musical instruments. One ad advertised flutes, violins, flageolets, music boxes, accordions, and "a bass drum, very little used, cheap." What could not be found in any of these well-stocked emporia could surely be found at Batchellor's Bazaar on lower Warren Street.

A Hudson lady who wanted to furnish her home could choose goods from C. Bame, just opposite city hall at Fourth and Warren Street, who sold and made to order "chairs, sofas, tables, bureaus, secretaries, and bedsteads." Equally useful was James Calkins at 284 Warren Street, who made and sold "wardrobes, side boards, dining, tea, center, card and ladies work tables, and hat-stands and French and other bed-steads," all of these in either mahogany or walnut and all "at the lowest prices."

A tea table could be had from Calkins, and an ornate sofa in the latest taste—with Grecian rolled arms and lions'-paw feet—could be purchased from Bame. A resplendent "gilt and framed looking glass" and a pair of girandoles ("the foremost mantle ornaments now in use") were offered at Hannah's. Mantle clocks were sold by C. E Butler at 323 Warren Street. What more could the elegant home need? Well, pictures for one thing. The *Washingtonian* opined, "There is no excuse for not having pictures when Nash is selling them at his Emporium for six shillings in nice gilt frames." On a more functional note, washing machines were available at George Parton's "furniture ware room" as well as a "Bates Portable Sliding Top Shower and Vapour Bath."

A profusion of confections could be had from the new bakery and confectionary that had just opened on Warren and claimed to have "the greatest variety of bread, cakes, and crackers ever offered in this city." Indeed, one could find there the riches of the sugary world: sugar and molasses cakes; pound cakes and gingerbread; fruit, sponge, and queen cakes; sugar jumbles, drop cakes, and ginger nuts. Wheat, cream, rye, and Indian bread were available, and all manner of crackers: butter, milk, water, sugar, graham, soda, and Boston. All of this Mr. Paul, the master baker, insisted was sold for prices "as low as any establishment in the state." To wash down these delights, green or black tea could be purchased from Robert Van Deusen at 320 Warren Street, at "the sign of the Chinese man."

At Wynkoop's Bookstore might be found a slim, leather-bound volume of Mr. Emerson's essays, a book of the inspirational sermons of Mr. Beecher, or J. P. R. James's *The Convict; or the Hypocrite Unmasked.* The daily paper had advertised the arrival at Wynkoop's of the Rev. George Smith's *Alamance, A Narrative of an Exploratory Visit to China and the Island of Hong Kong,* as well as the intriguing and perhaps even slightly scandalous (though ultimately morally uplifting) *The Fate of Infidelity,* by "A Converted Infidel." Or one might choose to read the newest *Godey's Lady's Book,* with drawings of the very latest fashions, as well as improving, juicy, and gossipy tales by Hudson's very own Alice B. Neal, author of the tantalizing *The Gossips of Rivertown.*

For relaxation there was the *Rural Repository,* one of Hudson's longest-running literary journals. There, edifying and heart-wrenching tales of unrequited love vied for attention with sentimental verse submitted by local poets on a perennially favorite subject—the death of fair but moral maidens: "But when I pressed her sweet lips twain, / And felt no kiss pressed back again: / And in her eye no tear could see, / When mine were flowing mournfully, / I knew her spirit fled."

The *Repository*'s pages included more weighty issues as well, such as a lengthy piece on the famines that were sweeping Europe and especially Ireland. The writer of the article made a connection between the famines and the political upheavals that were taking place throughout Europe, concluding that the "Hand of Providence" could be seen in these events, proving that it was an agency in the eternal applications of political and moral law. The article opined that the famines were one of the "means taken by the Almighty to ensure the true objects of political government" and suggested that terrible as they were, through them the peoples of Europe had been given a great choice "either to embrace the freedoms of America or embrace despotism." For when the hungry peoples of Europe were driven to America in search of food and work, then "the contemplative historian will register in Europe that the famines of 1846 and 1847 are among the causes of our progress, pointing out to the capitalist the numberless advantages and never failing resources of the land of Liberty."

A humorous little squib was used as filler at the end of the article: "Good Morning Mr. J___, where have you been keeping yourself this long time?" "Kept myself, I don't keep myself, I board on credit!" This was a quick jab at the economy of the times, when more people than ever before were depending on credit—a bad omen.

The *Columbia Washingtonian* carried that day in its foreign news column the information that the packet ship *Steven Whitney* had been lost with all hands on its voyage from New York City to Liverpool. On a far happier note the great paddle-wheel steamship *Britannia* was at long last within sight of Boston harbor. Most ominously, the English stock exchange was depressed because of "a formidable conspiracy which had been discovered in Paris." The market columns reported that there had been more mercantile failures and that the stock market was "dull as flour tended downward," wheat was "heavy and inactive," and cheese was "quiet." Then there was the sad intelligence that the composer Dr. Felix Mendelssohn Bartholdy had died in Leipzig at the age of thirty-nine.

The paper announced that the Franklin Library Association lecture hall on Union Street offered a lecture by Mr. Forster of Union College, and that some of the ladies of Hudson were conducting a fair to benefit the Hudson Orphan Asylum. The Hudson Sons of Temperance were to meet that night as well. To get to these edifying and salubrious events, one might purchase a new carriage from Mr. Chamberlain's carriage manufactory (as sound and well-sprung, it was to be hoped, as those that were once made at Mr. Delamater's carriage shop on the public square before the shop burned two years prior).

On the subject of the weather, we learn that the season has been unusually mild: "We would scarcely believe that yesterday was the 15th of December. No sign of winter yet. This weather is death on the muff and mitten business and wide awake to overshoes and umbrellas."

Marble fireplace mantles could be commissioned from the Hudson Marble factory on Warren just above the Farmer's Bank, where one might also commission a monument for oneself or a loved one. Price comparisons could be made at Hudson's other marble works, either Mr. Nicholson's Hudson Marble Works at Ferry Street, or Mr. Frizzell's Columbia Marble works in the Spaulding Building on Warren at the corner of Fourth Street. The latter promised to provide the "most satisfaction and at prices that cannot fail to suit." Such dark thoughts could fill one with a shiver of apprehension, unless comforted by the salutary admonition that one might have read in the *Rural Repository:* "Death is always an unspeakably great gain to a good man." It might be a great gain as well to Mr. Calkins, who advertised that in addition to tea tables and other furniture, he could also make coffins.

But behind this glittering façade of goods aplenty must have lingered a sense of unease as Hudsonians sought ways to save fading fortunes when the old maritime economy ended, perhaps by investing in the new miracles—steamboats and railroads. Some of these investments led only to further hardships for the city. Stephen B. Miller, writing in 1862, summed up the cumulative effect of Hudson's misfortunes at the midpoint of the nineteenth century: "Hudson was just then suffering, not so much from lack of enterprise, as from unsuccessful enterprise. The capital of its citizens, invested in the Hudson & Berkshire Rail Road, the whale fishery, the erection of the Hudson House and other enterprises, had nearly all been sacrificed, and two destructive fires had just brought additional loss to many of them, and thus under an accumulation of misfortunes every business interest had become depressed."[36]

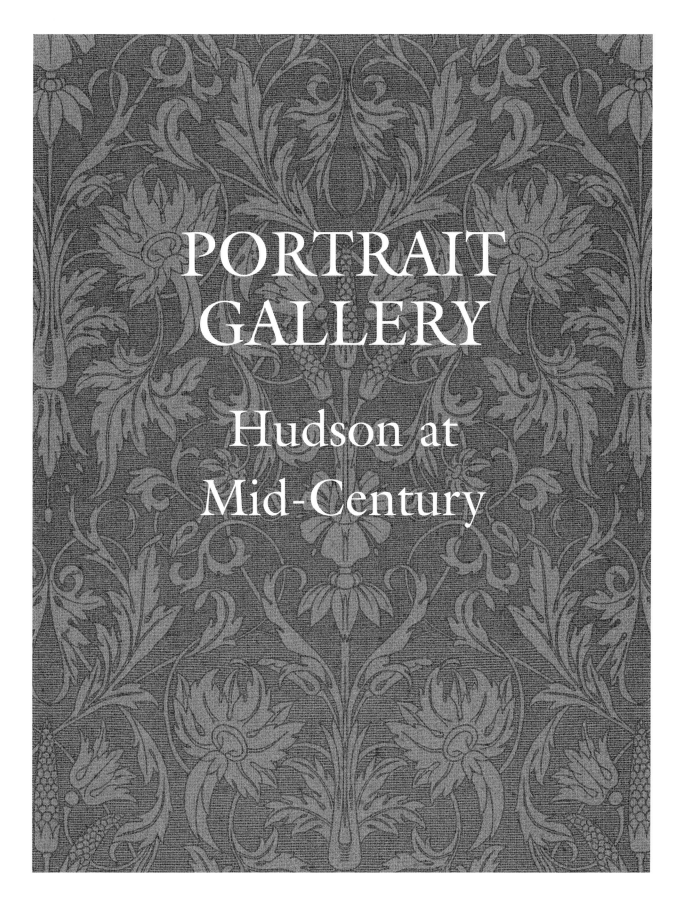

PORTRAIT GALLERY

Hudson at Mid-Century

The congregation of Christ Episcopal Church first met in the old schoolhouse that once stood on Diamond (Columbia) Street. They then built this brick church on Second and State Street, begun in 1795 and completed in 1802, and remained there until they moved to the present Christ Church on Washington Square. The Second Street building was then purchased by the Wesleyan Methodists, and in 1860 the Wesleyans and the members of the African Methodist Episcopal Zion Church united in one congregation and continued to worship together in this building.

The Hudson Academy, opened in 1807. Collection of Harry B. Halaco.

This elegant Federal brick building, possibly designed by Barnabas Waterman, was originally built for the First Universalist Society and Church of the City of Hudson about 1817. It was later sold to St. Mary's Parish and became St. Mary's School. It was located on the southwest corner of Allen and Third Street, and it burned in the late nineteenth century.

The first Columbia County Courthouse in the city of Hudson, built in 1835. A simple and elegant Greek Revival structure with a dome and six Ionic columns, this building located on Washington Square was torn down in 1900 to make way for the second Columbia County Courthouse in the city of Hudson.

The second church building of the First
Presbyterian Church of the City of Hudson,
built circa 1835–37 (photograph circa 1860).
The Presbyterians' first church had been built
at the corner of Second Street and Allen Street
(then Federal Street) in 1792. The congregation moved to the site of the old city courthouse
on the corner of Warren and Fourth when the
courthouse was demolished in 1835. There
they built a new church in the Gothic style, to
which they affixed the weathervane from the
first church.

The Reformed Church was built in the
Greek Revival style in 1836 and was located
on Warren below the corner of south Fifth
Street. The church was destroyed by fire in
the twentieth century.

St. Mary's Church (built circa 1847), Montgomery Street and Third Street in the 1860s.

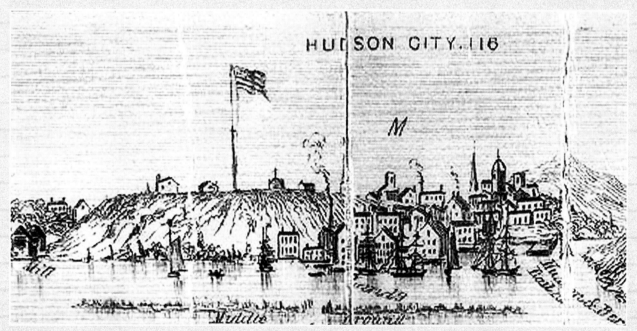

Panorama of the Hudson River from New York to Albany, *by Wade and Croomer, 1846. Courtesy of New York Public Library. This view of Hudson from the river in the 1840s shows the Flag House to the right of the flagpole on Parade Hill.*

Hudson and Warren Street in the 1840s, seen from Academy or Prospect Hill. Engraving by Barber and Howe, Historical Collections of New York, 1841. *Collection of the author.*

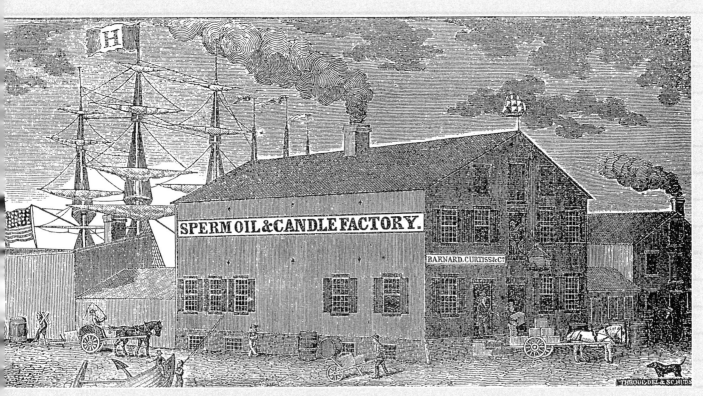

A sperm oil and candle factory in Hudson circa 1841. Engraving by Throop in the Rural Repository. *Collection of the Columbia County Historical Society, Kinderhook, New York.*

FOUR

WHO SHALL SAY THAT HUDSON IS
NOT ENJOYING THE ADVANTAGES
OF GREAT CHANGE?: 1850–1900

Hudson's whaling industry had finally come to an end, and though a period of adjustment was in order, a development had occurred that would set Hudson on a new and once-again prosperous economic course. In October 1841, after several years of planning and building, a railroad line had been opened between Hudson and Boston. Even as the end of the whaling and seagoing trade sealed the fate of one era—Hudson's shipbuilding, sailmaking, rope, oil and candle works, tanning, and wool mill industries had all failed by mid-century—the railroads and steamboats fostered the beginning of a new era, enabling new industries to open and Hudson to prosper once again.

Most people felt that the future clearly rode on the rails. The failure of the Hudson Berkshire Line in 1847 did not dampen what Margaret Schram called a "railroad frenzy." In 1851 more tracks were laid for the line from Albany to New York City that ran right along Hudson's waterfront. It seemed to bother no one that a railroad line now crossed the Great South Bay on a narrow landfill causeway.

Nor did anyone seem distressed that another incursion was made into the once-pristine South Bay. The Hudson Iron Company purchased about ninety acres of the bay and built the

Hudson Iron Works factory and iron smelting furnaces on pilings driven into the bed of the bay. The factory opened in 1851 and was the first heavy industry to contribute to the eventual disappearance of the South Bay. Ironically, one of the company's trustees was Elihu Gifford, father of Sanford Robinson Gifford, one of the Hudson River School painters who took as a subject the natural beauties of the landscape of the area, and whose pictures of the pristine South Bay are a telling counterpoint to later images of the bay that his father's factory helped destroy. As the factory produced its iron, the debris and cinders from the furnaces were thrown into the surrounding waters, thus gradually creating a landfill where the bay had been. The intention may have been to fill in the entire ninety acres as business increased. A woodcut of the period shows the factory sitting in the middle of the bay, with the railroad tracks running across it.

In the 1860s more heavy industries opened in the city. Hunt and Miller's Foundry made stoves. The Clapp and Jones Company made the Champion Steam Fire Engine, and C. H. Evans & Company was the first brewery opened in Hudson in the nineteenth century, with premises on Mill Street and also on State Street. Knitting mills and cotton mills were opened. Traver's Sash and Door Company, Clark's Clothing Factory, and Philips Spiral Corn Husker Company added to the list of manufacturing premises, as did Herbs' Tobacco Factory on Prospect Avenue near Warren Street, which processed tobacco both for export and for its cigar factory and sales store at 338 Warren Street.

Hudson was proud of its new industrial strength. Steamers docked at Hudson's waterfront, and money was coming in by rail as well. With money plentiful again, Hudsonians were moved once more to add their city. A new city hall was proposed, and in 1855 a grand new building in the Greek Revival style, designed by local architect William Avery, was opened to much fanfare. This building, on the corner of Warren and City Hall Place, housed the police station, the post office, the offices of the First National Bank, and the Common Council Chamber in which Hudson artist Henry Ary's portrait of Washington was displayed. The Franklin Library Association was now ensconced in the huge auditorium on the second floor. There it gave an extensive program of lectures, bringing many famous speakers to town including Henry Ward Beecher (father of Harriet Beecher Stowe, who would electrify the world with her novel, *Uncle Tom's Cabin*). Other notable lecturers were the abolitionist Wendell Philips and the spellbinding speaker Edward Everett, considered the greatest orator of his time. (Everett gave the main speech at the dedication of Gettysburg Battlefield. His oration lasted for two hours, after which Abraham Lincoln spoke for just a few minutes.)

It is also claimed that Ralph Waldo Emerson, who urged men to ignore the unreality of life's vicissitudes in favor of higher solutions, also spoke in Hudson—though some reports suggest that the great transcendentalist was prevented from reaching Hudson by a very real snowstorm. It is certain that Charles Dickens was not prevented from coming to Hudson, or so Alice B. Neal tells us in *The Gossips of Rivertown:* "The excitement occasioned by Charles Dickens passing through town" was so great that every time a traveler "with an uncommon quantity of long light hair" (as Dickens had) arrived at the Worth Hotel, "it was thought that it was surely Dickens himself again."

In the spirit of civic improvement, more schools were opened in Hudson to join the already successful and elegant Hudson Free Academy, opened in 1805 on a site near the cemetery and overlooking the city. In 1847 and 1848, Elizabeth and Sophie Peake saw a need for more extensive (and perhaps more cosmopolitan) education. In their Hudson Young Ladies Seminary they paid special attention to teaching French to Hudson's young ladies. In 1851, The Hudson Female Academy was opened in the building that had been first the Hudson Almshouse—a home for the city's poor—and then the Hudson Asylum for the Insane.

Hudson's religious groups built as well. The Methodists had previously built a brick church on their land at Third and Diamond streets. In 1853 they purchased the Friends' meeting hall (now the Boys and Girls Club) on Third Street between Union Street and Cherry Alley, and added a Gothic steeple. In 1857 Christ Episcopal consecrated their new church in the Gothic style on East Court and Union streets on Washington Square Park (which we now often call Court House Square). At about this time, the Reformed Church of Hudson—an offshoot of the Presbyterians—built a Greek Revival house of worship on the south side of Warren Street just below Fifth Street. By 1869 the Universalist Church had dedicated its Romanesque building across the street on the north side of Warren.

Henry Ary's portrait of George Washington, seen here hanging in the Common Council Chamber in old City Hall, now the Hudson Opera House. Collection of Hank and Debbie DiCintio.

In 1862 Stephen B. Miller, in *Sketches of Hudson,* gave us a picture of the city as he saw it then. It was as bright a depiction as Ignatius Jones's description in 1847 was grim:

We take our stand upon Parade Hill. Looking off, the same unequalled view of river and mountains which nothing human ever can change, still meets us; but around us all is different. The hill itself, instead of a naked rock, has been transformed into a pleasant and shaded resort, where the lover of the beautiful or the seeker after pleasure or health may comfortably linger in their search. From its base, instead of the gentle dashing of the waves, we hear the heavy rumbling of trains, and the shrill whistle, whose echo comes back thrice repeated by the opposite hills. Across the river's breast ... flits like a bird, one of the neatest and swiftest steam ferry boats upon the river. Should it be the latter part of the day, we shall see entering her wharf, returning from her daily trip to Albany, a fleet, beautiful little steamer, the *City of Hudson,* owned by Messrs. Power, Martin & Co., with groups of passengers upon her pleasant decks. At the same hour we shall see a

Warren Street from Fifth, looking west.

splendid steamer, either the *Oregon* owned by Messrs. Haviland, Clark & Co., or the *Connecticut*, by Messrs. Power, Bogardus & Co., boats in no particular second to any upon this or any other river, leaving for New York, and with a weight of freight and passengers which would call for the combined capacity of all the sloops of olden Hudson. Who shall say that in facilities for travel and business Hudson is not enjoying the advantages of great change?

Looking from the Southerly end of the hill, we see little beside the large store houses, to remind us of the ancient order of things in that portion of the city. Heavy fires, with the construction of the Hudson River Rail Road, have produced an entirely changed appearance. However, instead of "decayed wharves, ship-yards overgrown with grass" and "empty store-houses," we see a net-work of railroad tracks, trains constantly passing, depots, foundries, furnaces, etc., from which come sounds quite as indicative of life as the "gong of the rope-maker," or the "ring of the hammer." In the distance are the extensive works of the Hudson Iron Company, organized in 1849. … Nearer to us are those of the Columbia County Iron Company, the depot of the Hudson & Boston Railroad Company, organized upon the failure of the Hudson & West Stockbridge Rail Road Company, and now in successful operation—the extensive stove foundry of Messrs. Hunt & Miller—the depots of the Hudson River Rail Road Company—the works of the Hudson Gas Company—the freighting establishments of Haviland, Clark & Co., Power, Martin & Co., while upon the North side of the city stands the extensive brewery of Messrs. B. W. Evans & Co., and that of Messrs. Millard & Barnard—all giving employment to a large number of men, and furnishing good proof that this end of Hudson, although greatly changed in its business, is not entirely "dead."

Passing through Warren Street, we find it difficult to point out a residence or place of business which has not been modernized, greatly improved or wholly changed in external appearance. The same is true of Union, while the beautiful residences on Allen Street and vicinity, and at the head of the town, have all been built within a few years.

Turning to what is generally termed the business end of the city, we notice the extensive establishment of Mr. James Clark, for the manufacture of clothing—that of Messrs. Charles White & Co., for the manufacture of boots and shoes, the machine shop of C. H. Prentiss, the extensive furnace and adjoining works of Messrs. E. Gifford & Sons—all in ordinary times furnishing employment to many individuals. We find many spacious stores erected and scarcely one remaining not greatly enlarged and improved, indicating, and all of them doing, in times of general prosperity, an amount of business which, if stated, would not be believed by those who assert that "there is little or nothing done in Hudson."

Looking at our public buildings, we note still a greater change. The "shaky" houses of worship have all disappeared, and we see four new edifices erected within a few years, and two but a short time previous, so that every congregation now enjoys increased and comfortable church accommodations. The old Court House, deemed so disgraceful thirty years since, has given place to a fine marble structure, and we have added a City Hall at the cost of $27,000, capable of accommodating twelve hundred people, of which we justly have reason to be proud. We have in that period also erected a public house, an ornament to the city, and which, although for a while not meeting the expectation of its originators, is now in successful operation. We find the Press of the city all established with greatly enlarged and improved facilities for doing business; we see our streets well paved and well lighted with gas; we enjoy greatly increased water privileges; we have a Fire Department full and efficient, the pride of the city; and in every respect the equal of any other city; and in every particular, the Hudson of to-day, instead of being the "same old," is a very different and greatly improved place, from the Hudson of a quarter of a century ago.

Miller's proud descriptions do not prepare us for what is shown in period photographs of the bay. These show how during the later half of the nineteenth century the South Bay was being destroyed. The new railroad built across the bay blocked the movement of its waters, and riverfront industries, without foresight, built factories on landfills within the bay. At the height of the boom in the 1850s and 1860s, no one thought to question whether the bay was worth the trouble to save or whether the noise, smoke, and pollution could do harm.

PORTRAIT GALLERY

Enjoying the Advantages of Great Change
1850–1900

Hudson in the 1860s. Collection of the author.

View looking uptown on Warren Street from the Front Street entrance to the Promenade. This and the following images of Warren Street date from the mid-nineteenth century.

Historic Hudson ✦ An Architectural Portrait

South side of Warren Street below First Street looking downtown. The Waldron House, a Federal house possibly designed by Barnabas Waterman, is on the corner.

South side of Warren Street looking downtown from City Hall.

Historic Hudson ❋ An Architectural Portrait

South side of Warren at Fourth Street showing the Presbyterian Church and, in the foreground, Tilley and Aldcroft, clothiers.

A Walk on Warren Street

South side of Warren Street looking downtown from the corner of Fourth Street.

North side of Warren at Fourth Street, showing Davis Hall and in the foreground the building that housed the emporium of H. Rogers. The tall sign in front points the way to more downtown businesses.

North side of Warren Street above Fourth Street showing some of its elegant housing. None of the buildings in the foreground now remain.

South side of Warren above Fourth Street.

ᴄᴏ A Walk on Warren Street ᴏᴄ

*South side of Warren Street looking downtown
from the corner of Fifth Street.*

*North side of Warren looking downtown from the corner of Fifth Street,
showing the Universalist Church and street arcades.*

South side of Warren above Fifth Street looking uptown. The Central Hotel is in the right corner foreground.

⟳ A Walk on Warren Street ⟳

North side of Warren looking downtown from the corner of Sixth Street, circa 1880s. The corner building made way for the Hudson River Bank and is now the site of the NYS Division of Motor Vehicles.

∽ A Walk on Warren Street ∽

*South side of Warren below Seventh Street, showing the former Hudson
Arcade on the left and street arcades typical of the city at that time.*

A Walk on Warren Street

Looking down Warren from just above Seventh Street.

Opposite the Public Square on Warren between Park Place and Seventh Street in the 1860s, before the square was landscaped as park.

Union Street at Second Street in the 1860s. The Federal house visible on the left was probably designed by Barnabas Waterman. The Greek Revival colonnaded side porch was a later addition.

The Universalist Church, depicted here in a photograph from the early twentieth century, dedicated its new Romanesque-style house of worship on Warren below north Fifth Street in 1869. It is no longer a church and no longer has its steeple.

Columbia Street in the 1860s. The early Federal house on the left was once the law office of Martin Van Buren. It was razed in the twenty-first century to create a parking lot.

Laying cobblestones on Warren below Fifth Street in the 1860s.

Historic Hudson ⊛ An Architectural Portrait

Preparing for the laying of cobblestones on East Allen Street.

Laying cobblestones on Union below Fifth Street.

Methodist Episcopal Church, circa 1860s. This building standing on Third Street between Union Street and Cherry Alley may have incorporated some elements of the 1785 structure built on the site as the Quaker meetinghouse, Hudson's first house of worship. The Methodists acquired the site in 1854. The building, though much changed and with its steeple gone and decorative elements decayed or defaced, is now the Hudson Boys and Girls Club. Collection of Harry B. Halaco.

Methodist Episcopal Church, Hudson, N.Y.

Christ Church Episcopal on the corner of east Court and Union Street, across from Washington Square (which we now often call Court House Square), was designed by New York architect William G. Harrison and consecrated in 1857. It is an elegant structure in the Gothic Revival style. Its soaring steeple was removed in the early part of the twentieth century.

Allen Street off Washington Square in the 1860s—a tree-lined and fenced block of stately mansions.

Old City Hall, now the Hudson Opera House at Warren and City Hall Place. Designed by local architect William Avery in 1855 in the Greek Revival style, City Hall housed the police station, the post office, the offices of the First National Bank, and the chambers of the mayor and Common Council. The Franklin Library Association gave an extensive program of lectures in the huge auditorium on the second floor.

A Hudson fire truck in front of H. W. Rogers Hose.

Edmonds Hose, located on the park, in the 1860s.

A Hudson fire truck in the 1860s in front of Hoysradt Fire House on Warren above Fifth Street.

Hudson Iron Works. Engraving by Benson Lossing, The Hudson: From the Wilderness to the Sea, *1866.*

Hudson Iron Works, showing the train running on tracks raised on pilings in the bay. Collection of the author.

Historic Hudson ◉ **An Architectural Portrait**

Hudson Iron Works and the South Bay in the 1860s.

Hudson and the waterfront with Hudson Iron Works in the upper left.

Hudson's waterfront about 1860, with the Hudson Iron Works in the left background and the Hudson and Berkshire Railroad tracks running across the South Bay in the left corner.

The waterfront in the 1880s.

Historic Hudson ❊ An Architectural Portrait

*The South Bay
at the end of the
century.*

The South Bay.

Parade Hill, or the Promenade, showing Hudson's industrial waterfront.

Parade Hill, or the Promenade, in the late nineteenth century, showing the flagpole, a corner of the Flag House, and the Hudson City Light (Hudson–Athens Lighthouse), which was completed in 1874.

(Top left and right) Parade Hill, or the Promenade, in the 1860s.

Parade Hill, or the Promenade, in the 1860s, without fencing.

St. Winifred on Promenade Hill, after 1897. Collection of Harry B. Halaco.

Hudson in 1870.

Hudson in the 1880s.

THE DEPRESSION OF 1873

The rosy future that Miller's extravagant praise suggested lay ahead was to dissipate after the Civil War. In 1873 inflation, then depression, engulfed the nation and damaged Hudson, writing another chapter in what was by now a familiar cycle of boom and bust for the city. This depression was in part brought on by a lack of confidence in the new green demand notes issued by the Union government to help finance the Civil War. These "greenbacks," as they were called, were redeemable for gold, but many people feared that there would be no gold to redeem them. More importantly, a major economic reversal that began in Europe reached the United States in the fall of 1873. This was signaled in America by the failure of Jay Cooke and Company, the country's preeminent investment banking concern, which was the principal backer of many of the nation's railroads and which handled most of the government's wartime loans. Jay Cooke and Company's fall touched off a series of events that engulfed the entire nation. The New York Stock Exchange was closed for ten days. Credit dried up, foreclosures were common, and banks failed. Factories closed their doors, costing thousands of workers their jobs. Many businesses were unprepared for the sudden collapse. Years of overbuilding the nation's railroads had been accompanied by wild overspending. The failure of so many railroads led, of course, to a marked decline in railroad building, and that in turn affected firms that contributed to railroad construction, like iron mills.

This affected the Hudson Iron Works, one of the city's largest employers. Jobs were lost as orders for iron declined. This loss of jobs was to be exacerbated by the fire that destroyed the Columbia Iron Company later in the century. The domino effect brought closure to many Hudson businesses. For five years, times were hard. In the late 1870s it may have seemed to Hudsonians that a recovery of sorts was beginning, but in retrospect (as most economists now agree), the depression of 1873 was only the beginning of a longer depression that would last until the end of the century.

During a brief respite from the cycle of economic depressions in the 1880s, however, the city tried to forge ahead. Its famously muddy streets were paved with cobblestones. Perhaps to express confidence in the future, Promenade Hill (as Parade Hill was now called) was fenced and its walks and lawns were improved. Even the public square—which had languished for nearly a century as a barren and desolate space made even more uninviting by the fact that the tracks of the Berkshire and Albany Line had been run through it—received some trees. These were not planted by the city, but by private citizens who had grown weary of the eyesore in their midst and who had mounted a public subscription to create "a refreshing little oasis."[37] This oasis may not have provided uninterrupted refreshment, however, since trains of the Boston and Albany Railroad Company continued to pass through the park (the tracks are still there today).

The Depression of 1893

The brief recovery did not last long. In the 1890s a deep agricultural crisis threw the American South into depression. The shock hit Wall Street and urban areas in 1893 as part of a massive, worldwide economic crisis. One-quarter of the nation's railroads went bankrupt. In some cities, unemployment among industrial workers exceeded 25 percent. With almost 2.5 million people out of work and 500 banks and 16,000 businesses bankrupt, the depression of the 1890s was on a par with the Great Depression of the 1930s. By the end of the nineteenth century, the Hudson Iron Works closed for good and the factory was demolished, further adding to the dereliction of the South Bay. Some of the railroads that serviced Hudson went bankrupt, steamboat traffic went into decline, and Hudson's status as an important river port was finally lost. The South Bay itself, one of the Hudson Valley's great natural sites, the subject of many of America's greatest landscape painters, and one of the original keys to Hudson's prosperity, slowly became a swampy landfill clotted with the rusting detritus of failed and vanished industry.

Other changes had come to Hudson as well. Some Dutch was still spoken on Hudson's streets even into the early nineteenth century, but the city was largely a Protestant, English-speaking town and had its share of xenophobia. The industrialization of Hudson brought newcomers aplenty to Hudson's streets. Irish, Polish, and some Italian immigrants had come to America ever since the mid-nineteenth century. Many came to Hudson as well. Irish moved into Hudson in the late 1840s to work on the railroads, and Italians came later to work in the brickyards. Hudson's demographics began to change. By the 1870s Hudson was no longer a nearly homogenous, Anglo-Dutch, white community.

The influx of new people brought change to Hudson's religious communities. St. Mary's Roman Catholic Church was founded as early as 1847, signaling the end of the Protestant monopoly in Hudson, and by the 1870s, St. Mary's had a parish of more than 600 people. By 1899 the parish had built its own school, St. Mary's Academy. While African–Americans had always lived in Hudson (some as slaves), little is known of the very early days of their community. In 1855 the Zion Methodist Episcopal Church was founded and eventually occupied a building on Second and State Street formerly owned by Christ Episcopal. In 1872, St. John's Methodist Episcopal Church was formed, and the two African–American churches had a combined membership of nearly 200 people. In 1868, Hudson's first synagogue was located on Diamond Street between Fifth and Sixth streets, and by the turn of the century there were two Jewish congregations. In 1907, Hudson's Italian community built a Catholic church for their own use. Anna Bradbury wrote in 1910 that the new cement plants employed "almost exclusively foreign and colored labor." She notes in her summary that this is "an unsuspected foreign element in the city which is of comparatively recent growth."[38]

To this increasingly diverse city a statue of St. Winifred, patron of virgins, was given in 1896 by General William De Peyster, who said that he knew Hudson had room for one more saint. The twelve-foot bronze statue was erected on Promenade Hill. Winifred was a Welsh princess and a devout Christian who was beheaded for her recalcitrance after resisting the advances of Prince Caradoc. Legend has it that her head rolled down a hill and a holy well flowed from where it came to rest. Hudson, no longer virginal, may have needed her help. And perhaps it was given. Beginning in 1897, Hudson, along with the rest of the nation, began to see a gradual recovery and a slow return to prosperity.

Hudson's Architecture: Gothic Revival, Italianate, and Second Empire, 1850–1900

In the late 1850s various styles of architecture—generally imprecisely known as Victorian—gained popularity. Among the first styles to succeed and sometimes to supplant the classic formality of Greek Revival was the romantic and exuberant Gothic Revival. The most obvious characteristics of this style, which recalls the Gothic architecture of European cathedrals and castles, are the pointed arches, high, pointed gabled roofs, vaults, gothic tracery and motifs, and the use of natural building materials—wood and stone—to interpret the style. Interiors displayed the same complex forms, elaborate detailing, multi-textured and multicolored walls—in short, all the architectural and design vernacular typical of the "Gothic taste," as the age described the style that had first been introduced to America in the early nineteenth century by Benjamin Latrobe. Latrobe had designed the city of Washington D.C. in the classical style, but by the 1820s he began to incorporate Gothic motifs into his other work. The style was employed in so-called Gothic cottages by American architect Alexander Jackson Davis and by Andrew Jackson Downing, the architect and garden designer who popularized the Gothic in his book Cottage Residences (1842). Richard Upjohn's Gothic churches in New York City defined the style and made Gothic the style of choice for American churches for a century.

Some Gothic-style "cottages" were built in Hudson—one on Union Street just below Seventh Street, and another on Allen Street. A third, at 59 Allen Street, may have been designed by A. J. Davis for Charles Alger, the owner of the Hudson Iron Works. Christ Episcopal Church on east Court Street, built in 1854–1857 and designed by New York City architect William G. Harrison, is Hudson's best example of the style. The present Presbyterian Church at the corner of Fourth and Warren streets was first built in an early Gothic Revival style in 1837 and incorporated the weathervane (now reproduced), marble threshold, and town clock from the congregation's first church on Federal (Allen) Street. The Warren Street church originally had a single center steeple, "rather squat and ugly" some thought, but an 1875 renovation resulted in the present, soaring steeple. It is believed that John A. Wood was the architect for the new façade. Hudson's other Gothic church, on Sixth and Warren streets, is the German Lutheran Church, built in Carpenter Gothic style and designed by Michael O'Connor.

Another sub-style of "Victorian" architecture developed at the same time as the Gothic. Italianate style appeared in the United States in the early 1840s and was also popularized by the pattern books of Andrew Jackson Downing. This style dominated American houses constructed between 1850 and 1890. It drew upon Italian country villas for inspiration, as well as upon Renaissance buildings described and drawn by English travelers visiting Europe on "Grand Tour" pilgrimages in the late eighteenth and early nineteenth century. Characterized by cupolas, prominent eaves supported by heavy brackets, low, sloping roofs, verandas, and often towers, these houses were intended to be "picturesque" as well as romantically evoking old Europe. By the late 1860s this style had completely overshadowed its earlier companion, Gothic Revival.

Italianate villas appeared in the Hudson Valley, and several in Hudson itself, including the Terry–Gillette Mansion at 601 Union Street, built circa 1850 after a design by architect Richard Upjohn. The Wallace Hannah House on south Fifth and Partition

Street is another fine example. It was constructed by Hannah, a builder responsible for several other houses on the street. At about the same time, A. J. Davis's daybook indicates that he also designed the refitting and expansion in the Italianate style of the John Gaul House—the house that was once the parsonage for the First Presbyterian Church on south Fourth Street at the corner of Union.

In the 1860s still another style swept America, which was seeking something imposing and imperial to reflect the nation's expansive gilded age. This was the Second Empire style, so-called because it imitated the building fashions of France's Second Empire over which Napoleon III presided. Second Empire style came to the United States after the Paris Exhibition in 1855, and soon the boxy mansard rooflines (named after the seventeenth-century French architect Francois Mansart) and dormer windows—and later, side or central villa-like towers, molded cornices, and decorative brackets beneath the eaves—became the necessary hallmarks of any building that wanted to be considered the latest and most modern thing in architecture. In Hudson, grand homes in the private and gated Willard Place were built in this style, as were the imposing Farmer's Bank on Warren Street and the Elk's Club on lower Warren. The bank and the club are long gone, while Willard Place is sadly degraded.

The 1860s also saw the development of the so-called stick style, a transitional style linking the earlier Gothic Revival style with the later Queen Anne style. Stick-style houses typically have a steeply gabled roof, often with steeply pitched cross gables. Decorative trusses at the apex of gables are also distinguishing features, and sunbursts or texture in the gables are common features. Some stick-style houses have a square or rectangular tower with a pyramidal hip roof. Porches are another regular feature, usually with shed roofs supported by diagonal or curved braces.

A variety of styles was exhibited in newly built Hudson houses after 1880. These included Queen Anne, the Romanesque (as developed in buildings by H. H. Richardson), High Victorian Gothic and, in a return to its stylistic roots, the Colonial Revival.

These revival styles replaced Second Empire in popularity. Dominant characteristics of Queen Anne are a steeply pitched roof of irregular shape, usually with a front-facing gable, patterned shingles, cutaway bay windows, and other architectural devices to avoid a smooth-walled appearance. The Richardson Romanesque style most often was used for churches and other public structures such as city halls, schools, and courthouses. In Hudson the best examples of the style were the Hudson Armory and the Fourth Street School (now demolished). Romanesque houses are always built of masonry and usually have rough-faced, squared stonework and wide, rounded Romanesque arches at windows, porches, and entrances. The Colonial Revival style did not replicate the Georgian and Federal styles; rather, it produced free interpretations of those styles. Palladian windows are a frequent feature of Colonial Revival houses, as are cornices decorated with modillions or dentils, elaborate broken pediments over windows and doors, pilasters, door surrounds with sidelights and sometimes fanlights, and decorative medallions and swags.

The city saw the work of two native architects during this time. One was Henry S. Moul; the other was Michael J. O'Connor. Both worked in an eclectic style with overtones of the Romanesque and designed Hudson buildings at the end of the nineteenth century and into the early twentieth century. Moul was born in Victor, New York, of Hudson Valley Dutch descent. He moved to Hudson in 1875 and, two years later, commenced an apprenticeship to learn the carpenter's trade with James E. McClure. In 1894 he formed a partnership with Frank B. Lasher under the name of H. S. Moul and Company, Carpenters and Builders. Moul was responsible for the design of numerous residences at the turn of the twentieth century, including 461 East Allen and 39 West Court Street, built after 1894 for John F. X. Brennen. It appears that Moul built this house from a design by O'Connor. Other Moul buildings include the Columbia County Courthouse (1900, burned in 1907), the Anshe Emeth Synagogue (1909, now the Shiloh Baptist Church), and 445 Warren Street, an unusual building that was designed by Moul as his home and office. The building comprises two stories on the east side, three on the west, and an elegantly framed entry in a central bay topped by a balcony tower. Fine woodwork, stained glass, and molded brickwork add surface richness to this complex design.

Few architects have had a more profound effect on Hudson than Michael J. O'Connor (1851–1933), born in Waterford, New York. O'Connor attended, but did not graduate from, Polytechnic Institute (now Rensselaer Polytechnic Institute) at Troy. He began his career in Saratoga Springs, but moved to Hudson in 1879. For a half century O'Connor was the primary architect for many private houses and public buildings, including the Fireman's Home, Emmanuel Lutheran Church, and the Sixth Street and Allen Street schools.

The nineteenth century saw a remarkably inventive diversity in American architectural styles. While many small towns either allowed these trends to pass them by or found one particular style that suited them best, Hudson's architects, builders, and residents seem to have embraced that diversity. Houses and public buildings in Hudson were constructed in every major American architectural style, and substantial numbers of them have survived.

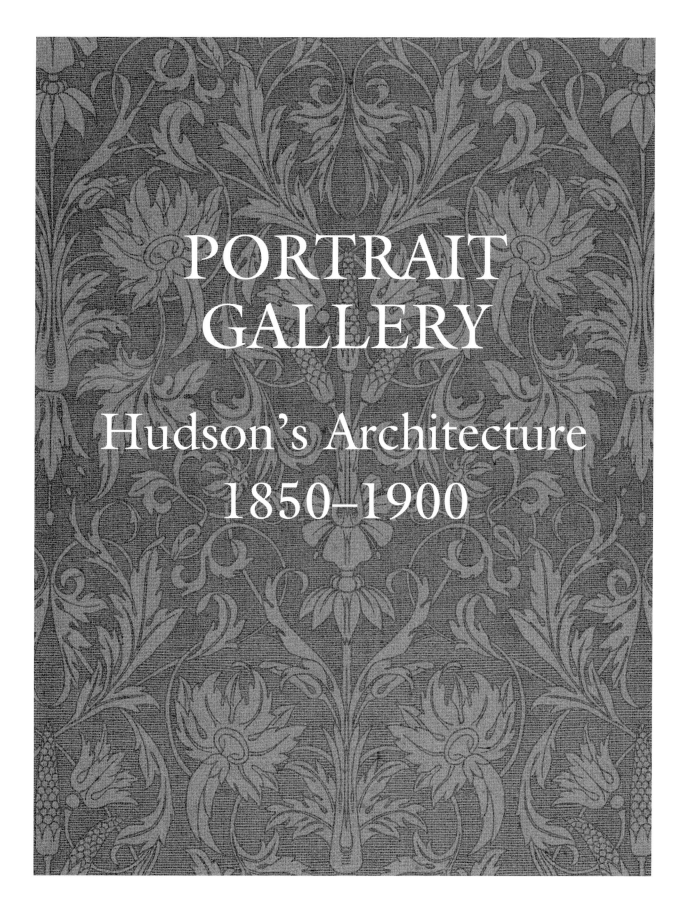

PORTRAIT GALLERY

Hudson's Architecture
1850–1900

Gothic Revival house on Allen Street, about 1940.

This Gothic Revival house at 59 Allen Street may have been designed by A. J. Davis for Charles Alger, the owner of the Hudson Iron Works

Christ Church with its Gothic Revival steeple intact.

ꙮ Gothic Revival ꙮ

*The façade of the First Presbyterian Church
was remodeled in the Gothic Revival style by
John A. Wood circa 1875.*

German Lutheran Church on Sixth Street between Warren and Columbia Street, built in Carpenter Gothic style to a design by Michael O'Connor in the 1880s.

～Gothic Revival～

The gothic spire of the First Presbyterian Church rises above the city. To the left is the tower of the Methodist Church (now the Hudson Boys and Girls Club). This was eventually removed. A zeppelin floats above, which dates this photo after 1900.

Italianate Villas

The Terry–Gillette Mansion at 601 Union Street was built in the Italianate villa style circa 1850 after a design by architect Richard Upjohn.

The Wallace Hannah house on south Fifth and Partition Street is another fine example of the Italianate villa style. Hannah was a local builder and responsible for several houses on South Fifth Street.

Italianate Villas

The John Gaul House, once the parsonage for the First Presbyterian Church, on South Fourth Street at the corner of Union Street. A. J. Davis's daybook indicates that he designed the refitting and expansion of the John Gaul House in the Italianate style.

Second Empire

The Second Empire Farmer's Bank, formerly on the north side of the 500 block of Warren Street. The building was destroyed by fire.

A Second Empire house on Willard Place.

The Elks Club on Warren below Second Street stood on the present site of Thurston Park. Destroyed by fire.

Stick Style, Queen Anne and Romanesque

Stick-style Victorian house built on Cross Street by Hudson architect Henry Moul for Miss A. Limbrick. Destroyed by fire.

Romanesque row house on lower Warren Street.

Queen Anne-style houses located on Allen Street. Collection of Hank and Debbie DiCintio.

The Romanesque Fourth Street School at the corner of Fourth and State Street, designed by Henry Moul. The building was demolished.

Stick Style, Queen Anne and Romanesque

The Romanesque Armory on North Fifth Street, photo 1930s.

The Sixth Street School, designed by Michael J. O'Connor. Collection of Hank and Debbie DiCintio.

⌒Stick Style, Queen Anne and Romanesque⌒

The Allen Street School, designed by Michael J. O'Connor.

The Fireman's Home, designed by Michael J. O'Connor.

Stick Style, Queen Anne and Romanesque

The 1906 Morgan Jones House on Allen Street at Willard Place, designed in the Dutch Jacobean style by Albany architect Marcus Reynolds.

The second Columbia County Court House in Hudson, located on Washington Square Park, designed by Henry Moul. Built in 1900; burned in 1907.

The present Columbia County Courthouse, built in 1907 and designed by Warren and Wetmore, the architects of Grand Central Station. Photograph taken in the 1930s.

∽ Classical Revival ∾

Another Warren and Wetmore building, at the corner of Warren Street and Sixth Street. Collection of Hank and Debbie DiCintio.

A Classical Revival building, built as a bank, now Hudson City Hall. Collection of Hank and Debbie DiCintio.

FIVE

THE CITY WAS MERELY DOZING:
HUDSON, 1900–1930

I n 1905 a book called *Illustrated Hudson* bravely announced that the Hudson of 1905 was no longer a "finished city"—a reference, of course, to the effects on Hudson of the depression of the 1890s. On the contrary, the book says: "The city was merely dozing because the citizens had become sluggish and inactive in their regard for its highest welfare. What was needed during those years of municipal laziness, and what has since been applied, to the great benefit of the community, was an awakening, a spurring, to goad the city on to its earlier life and activity." To blame the people of the city, rather than the larger economic forces of the times, was a misreading of the situation.

To illustrate their point that Hudson was on the move again, the authors described the city's businesses in some detail. Of the ninety or so commercial enterprises they mention, only a handful dated back to the middle years of the nineteenth century, a dozen had appeared in the 1860s and 1870s, more than half were founded after the late 1880s, and the rest were started up after 1900. Thus, despite the age of the city, most of Hudson's businesses in 1905—and these consisted primarily of shops on Warren Street—were barely thirty years old. There were now few heavy industries, and most predated the turn of the century. The Gifford–Wood Company did general foundry work and was Hudson's oldest surviving business, established as the Gifford

Company in 1814. Hudson City Brewing was established in 1905, but was the successor to the Granger Brewing Company, established in 1855. The Hudson Fibre Company produced cotton and wool and battings for upholstery, and was established in 1892. The Union Mills made cotton and wool shirts and drawers, and was established in 1880. One exception was the huge Portland Cement Company, which mined limestone from the hills above Hudson. It was built in 1903 on the site of the old Hudson Iron Works on the South Bay and was Hudson's newest, largest, and heaviest industry, coming just after the economic tide had turned and Warren Street had begun to thrive again.

Illustrated Hudson's list of commercial establishments suggests that everything one needed could be found in Hudson in 1905. To provide for the dining table, Warren Street boasted fourteen groceries, four confectionary shops, at least two butchers, a fish and oyster shop, a wine and liquor merchant, the Great Atlantic and Pacific Tea Company, the Union Pacific Tea Company, and a purveyor of fruits and nuts. Drugs and patent medicines could be obtained from three pharmacies. McKinstry's still sold Rossman's Celebrated Pile Cure and Hardy's Elixir, as well as Magic Fluid for the hair. Five tobacco shops offered tobacco, pipes, and cigars (domestic and Havana). There were four tailors, including Tilley and Aldcroftt, then one of Hudson's oldest businesses (established 1856). Men's hats could be had at 437 Warren Street at Guinan's, and women's hats were to be found at The Bouquet at 513 Warren Street. Shoes were available at two stores, both owned by the Klines. Four large variety and dry goods establishments sold almost everything. There were several hotels—including the Worth, the St. Charles, the Lincoln, the Germania, and the Portland—and several restaurants, including Wolfs Café, in business since 1865. Wolfs had a bar where "stimulating beverages" were served as well as a good dinner.

Perhaps it was at Wolfs that Henry James, the American novelist, had dinner during his visit to the city in 1905. He arrived, as Anna R. Bradbury writes, in an automobile "with two ladies and a French poodle." One of the ladies was no doubt James's inseparable traveling companion, the redoubtable novelist Edith Wharton. When they went to the Worth Hotel for dinner, as James himself described it in *The American Scene,* they "encountered coldness at the door of the main hotel by reason of our French poodle." When they were told that poodles were not welcome at the Worth, James and his party "found dinner at a cook shop." James dismissed with frigid tranquility the doorkeeper at the Worth who, he opined, had a mind "indifferent to the opportunity of intercourse … with fine French poodles." James and Wharton did not leave Hudson without some praise, however, for the "hospitality of the cook shop was touchingly, winningly, unconditional."[39] Bradbury sniffingly dismisses James's comments about her beloved Hudson as merely exhibiting "the smallness of the great Analyst." It is perhaps lucky for Bradbury—whose own account is not occasionally without pettiness—that she did not that evening encounter either James, looking for material for *The American Scene,* or that other incomparable analyst of social pretension, Edith Wharton.

On Warren and off, individual businesses sold stoves, harnesses, carriages, curtains, paint, root beer and soda, cola and ice, hay and feed, and leather goods. There were two plumbers, a carpenter, an electrician, the First National Bank, architect Henry S. Moul, barbers and shaving parlors, two newspapers—*The Evening Register* and the *Hudson Morning Republican*—and Jones Insurance agents in their offices in the grand Second

Empire–style Farmer's Bank building on Warren. After death, needs were supplied by two undertakers and Nicholson Monuments (almost the oldest business in Hudson, established in 1835). Cedar Park Cemetery, which had remained untended and desolate until 1872, was landscaped and fenced in 1896 and provided with ornamental gates just in time to welcome new arrivals from the new century.

Unfortunately, Hudson's latest cycle of prosperity did not last long. The nation moved quickly from boom to bust and back again. In the early twentieth century many hoped that economic prominence might return to Hudson with the beginning of cement production in the city. And, indeed, cement did become Hudson's largest industry for the next half century. Limestone mined from the hills above Hudson was processed on the site of the defunct Hudson Iron Works where the South Bay once existed. A downturn in the national economy occurred in 1908 and may have contributed to the closing of the Hudson Portland Cement Company, with the loss of 300 jobs. In 1910, after a two-year hiatus, cement manufacturing began again when the Atlas Cement Company purchased and dismantled the Portland waterfront plant and built a new, inland mill closer to the quarry in Greenport. In 1911 the Knickerbocker Cement Company began operations on the north side of Becraft Mountain. By 1913 about 1,200 people worked in the two plants. Hudson's main street seemed to thrive again.

The economy revived again after World War I, but as was the case after the Civil War, decline followed revival. In 1921 another sharp downturn occurred that many economists believe was an early signal of the Great Depression of 1929. By the mid-1920s, Hudson's economy was almost entirely dependent on one industry alone—the cement plants. The mills had closed and Prohibition (1920–1933) had brought an end to C. H. Evans & Co. Brewery. The city had, in effect, become a company town. Then came the Great Depression in 1929.

Neither Hudson nor America would recover from the Great Depression for more than a decade. Hudson's economy revived a little during and after World War II, and some period photographs show a busy Warren Street. Other photographs suggest a different story, with signs in Warren Street shop windows announcing a store for rent or a shop going out of business, rather than advertising merchandise. Streets off Warren are empty, houses are desolate, and the pavement is in disrepair—all signs of neighborhoods in decay.

MODERN JEZEBELS: HUDSON, 1930S–1950S

One industry did continue to flourish and even expand, however. It was during this time that Hudson's long-established houses of prostitution became Hudson's largest tourist attraction, supported by a tolerant and self-perpetuating political machine and an indulgent police force. Hudson's name became a byword not for commerce, but for vice. What had been founded as a Quaker town in the eighteenth century became known as the Northeast's bordello in the twentieth. Prostitution flourished on Hudson's infamous Diamond Street in brothels that were visited by men from all over the region, the state, and even the nation.

Hudson's houses of ill fame were not a product of the 1930s. They had probably always been there, as Bruce Hall suggests in *Diamond Street: The Story of the Little Town with the Big Red Light District.* Indeed, as early as the 1840s people complained to the Common Council about riotous doings on Diamond Street, and in that same year the Columbia Washingtonian angrily condemned Mrs. Betsy Smith as a "modern Jezebel" for bringing her fourteen-year-old niece into her "house of some sort of fame." The niece was not repentant, but when harassed by the worthy ladies of the temperance society she did provide them with a list of names of Hudson men who had "visited her during her moments of frailty." The Common Council ruminated a few days later about the "numerous houses of ill fame with which our city is disgraced," but ruminate seems to be all they did.

Hudson's first anti-vice ordinance was not enacted until 1859, when it was decreed that anyone keeping a brothel or gambling house could be fined $25. Hall follows the wayward path of Hudson's illicit nightlife down through the decades, and chronicles the inaction of compliant and complicit city governments that did nothing about the situation and profited from vice. Finally, something was done. In a single day in 1950, a spectacular state police raid ordered by Governor Thomas Dewey shut down the city's brothels and gambling dens. Many of Hudson's politicians and some of its police were arrested, and its famous madams and their "soiled doves" were sent packing. With prostitution gone, Hudson had little left to offer save for an undoubtedly shame-faced St. Winifred whose powers of protection, in Hudson at least, had surely failed.

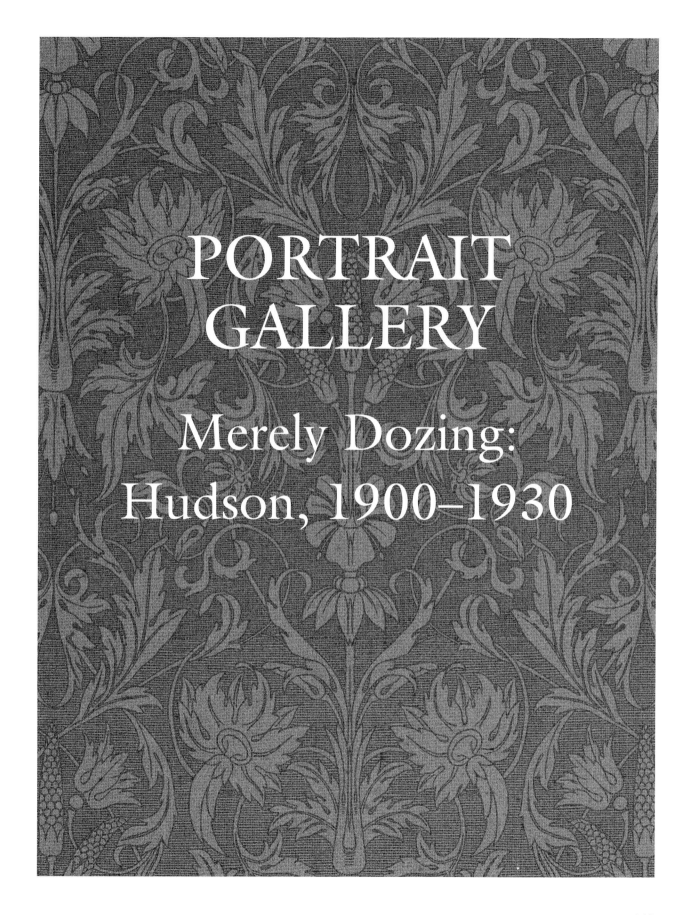

PORTRAIT GALLERY

Merely Dozing: Hudson, 1900–1930

Warren Street, looking East, Hudson, N.Y.

South side of Warren Street above Front Street. This and the following images of Warren Street date from circa 1900. Collection of Harry B. Halaco.

A Walk on Warren Street ca.1900

WARREN ST. & WORTH HOUSE, HUDSON, N.Y.

South side of Warren Street below Third Street looking uptown, with Worth Hotel. Collection of Harry B. Halaco.

Warren Street looking downtown with old City Hall on the left. The Federal Hathaway House can just be seen at center right. Collection of Harry B. Halaco.

South side of Warren Street at City Hall Place, looking uptown. Collection of Harry B. Halaco.

ELK THEATRE, WARREN ST., HUDSON, N.Y.

North side of Warren Street looking uptown across from City Hall Place. Note the Rialto Theater on the left. Collection of Harry B. Halaco.

A Walk on Warren Street ca.1900

North side of Warren Street above Fourth Street with the Evans Mansion on the right. Collection of Harry B. Halaco.

A Walk on Warren Street ca.1900

Warren Street from Hotel Central,
Hudson, N. Y.

Warren Street looking downtown near the corner of Fifth Street. The Central Hotel is on the left. Collection of Harry B. Halaco.

Warren Street below Fourth Street looking uptown from mid-block. Collection of Harry B. Halaco.

Warren Street at mid-500 block looking downtown towards Fifth Street. Collection of Harry B. Halaco.

❧ A Walk on Warren Street ca.1900 ❧

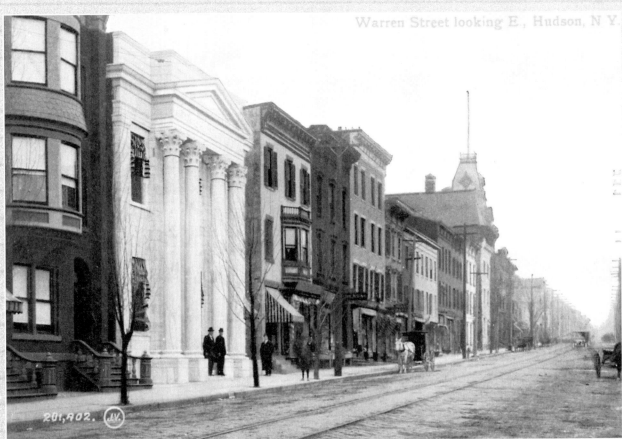

Warren Street in the 500 block looking uptown towards Sixth Street. Collection of Harry B. Halaco.

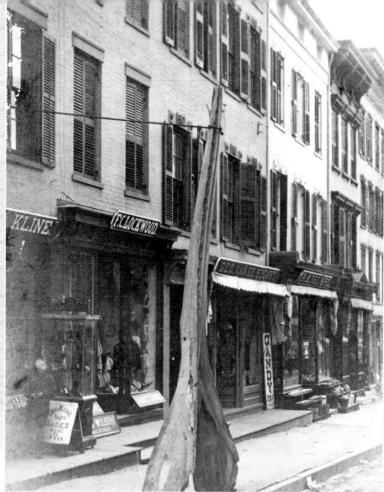

The whale's jaw, seen here at Kline's shop on Warren Street above Fifth, was long displayed in Hudson. Photograph circa 1910.

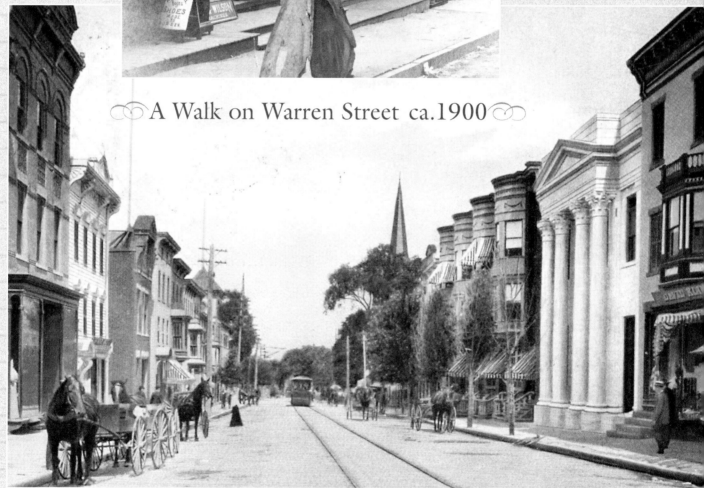

A Walk on Warren Street ca.1900

Warren Street looking downtown towards Fifth Street. Collection of Harry B. Halaco.

Warren Street at mid-500 block looking uptown towards Sixth Street. Collection of Harry B. Halaco.

∽ A Walk on Warren Street ca.1900 ∽

Warren Street looking downtown from corner of Sixth Street. The Federal house on the left was on the site of the present Bank of America. Collection of Harry B. Halaco.

The Public Square in 1905. Collection of Harry B. Halaco.

Public Square, Hudson, N.Y.

A Walk on Warren Street ca.1900

Worth House, Hudson, N. Y.

The Worth House, built in 1836, was located on the south side of Warren Street halfway down the block below Third Street. It was demolished in the twentieth century by the city of Hudson. Collection of Harry B. Halaco.

The Farmers (now St. Charles) Hotel across from the Public Square.

Historic Hudson ◉ An Architectural Portrait

The Hotel Portland/Waldron House stood on the south side of Warren Street at the corner of First Street and was demolished with the entire block in an urban renewal project.

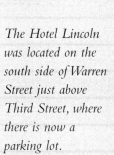

The Hotel Lincoln was located on the south side of Warren Street just above Third Street, where there is now a parking lot.

Union Mills on the corner of north Sixth and Washington streets.

The Evans Ale Brewery was located on Mill Street.

On the waterfront.

Beginning as one of Hudson's hotels, this early-nineteenth-century building was converted to a warehouse and later demolished. Collection of Hank and Debbie DiCintio.

The Hudson waterfront from the Promenade about 1900. Collection of Harry B. Halaco.

The Hudson waterfront in 1908. Collection of Hank and Debbie DiCintio.

Historic Hudson ● **An Architectural Portrait**

The Hudson–Athens Ferry slip in the early twentieth century.

Permanent lodging—Cedar Park Cemetery.

∽ Hudson in the 1920s and 1930s ∽

Warren Street below Seventh Street in the 1920s. Collection of Harry B. Halaco.

Hudson in the 1920s and 1930s

South side of Warren Street looking uptown from just below Sixth Street in the late 1920s.

*South side of Warren Street looking downtown
from Seventh Street in the late 1920s.*

Hudson in the 1920s and 1930s

*Depression: going
out of business in the
1930s. Collection of
Jeremiah Rusconi.*

Closed for the duration, 1930s. Collection of Jeremiah Rusconi.

Hudson in the 1920s and 1930s

Depression: the corner of North Fifth and Columbia Street in the 1930s. Collection of Jeremiah Rusconi.

Warren Street at north First Street in the 1930s. Collection of Hank and Debbie DiCintio.

ᴏᴐHudson in the 1920s and 1930sᴐᴏ

Warren Street at Third Street in the 1930s. Collection of Hank and Debbie DiCintio.

Historic Hudson ❈ **An Architectural Portrait**

Delivering Evans Ale to John Wolf's tavern on City Hall Place. Collection of Hank and Debbie DiCintio.

⌒ Memories of Old Hudson ⌒

Delivering ice on lower Warren Street. Collection of Jeremiah Rusconi.

*An early Hudson
Federal house on
the corner of South
Front and Allen.*

❧ Memories of Old Hudson ❧

*Collection of
Jeremiah Rusconi.*

Memories of Old Hudson

Two of Hudson's popular bars. The Crystal (top) was next to the former VFW building across from old City Hall. Collection of Jeremiah Rusconi.

Speed's Bar was in the 300 block of Warren Street. Collection of Jeremiah Rusconi.

Memories of Old Hudson

The Hudson Grill was on Warren Street, just off the corner of Seventh Street across from the park. Collection of Jeremiah Rusconi.

The Hotel Lincoln, on the south side of Warren Street above Third Street, was demolished to make way for the present municipal parking lot.

Collection of
Jeremiah Rusconi.

Memories of Old Hudson

*Hudson Institutions: The interior of La Bella Napoli, eventually to be Bucci's, and later the Charleston.
Collection of Jeremiah Rusconi.*

Hudson Institutions: Brandow's Restaurant on lower Warren Street near old City Hall. Collection of Jeremiah Rusconi.

Hudson institutions: Sam's Food market. Collection of Jeremiah Rusconi.

SIX

A FINISHED CITY:
HUDSON, 1950s–1970s

During the next two decades the two cement plants closed. The Knickerbocker cement plant closed in 1967, in part because it was decided that limestone reserves did not remain in sufficient quantities in the Becraft Hills to justify an expensive renovation of the plant. Union problems and environmental restrictions had added greatly to the plant's financial difficulties. In 1976, Universal Atlas Cement was purchased by Saint Lawrence Cement whose subsidiary, Independent Cement, carried on manufacture in Hudson for a brief period, closing in 1977. The end of cement manufacturing at these two plants resulted in a loss of 450 jobs.

By the mid-1970s Hudson seemed empty of hope. Its economy was blasted and its population was in decline. A large welfare constituency filled the city's tenements. Hudson was virtually a ghost town. Its property values sank to such low levels that its elegant nineteenth-century houses could be purchased for as little as $20,000. Warren Street—Hudson's bustling main street for 200 years—was filled with empty and abandoned stores. The eight-block-long commercial thoroughfare boasted only a handful of occupied shops. Warren Street's decline was a familiar plight to nearly every small town in America. Never entirely recovering from the Great Depression, further damaged by the closing of Hudson's two cement plants, and finally unable to compete with chain stores in the mall, Hudson's mom-and-pop stores went out of business. Main Street America—as typified by Warren Street's small, family run shops—had become a thing of the past.

There were few restaurants and no venues for music or art—not even a movie house. The city was perceived by its neighbors to be crime-ridden and dangerous. Hudson's streets emptied of people. A somnolence fell on the town. Hudson moved slowly, despairingly, very nearly to the brink of economic and social disaster. By the end of the 1970s, the former "miracle city" desperately needed a miracle.

HUDSON'S ARCHITECTURE IN THE TWENTIETH CENTURY

In the new century, Hudson did not witness a burst of new construction comparable to that of some periods of the nineteenth century, but construction did continue. In fact, nationally known architects designed buildings for Hudson in the twentieth century Two of these structures are in the Academic (also known as Classical Revival or Beaux Arts) style, which was a favored style of the times for museums, railroad terminals, court-houses, and government buildings. Both were designed by the architectural firm of Warren and Wetmore, the architects responsible for Grand Central Terminal in New York City. The Columbia County Courthouse (1908) on Washington Square at Union Street is a Warren and Wetmore building, as is the former headquarters of the Hudson City Savings Institution at the corner of Sixth and Warren Street, where the Department of Motor Vehicles and other county offices are now located. Another important early-twen-tieth-century building in Hudson is the Colonial Revival structure at 544 Warren Street, which once housed Fleet Bank. It was designed by Shreve and Lamb, the architects who designed the Empire State Building.

It was not construction, but demolition, however, that had the greatest effect on Hudson's architecture in the early twentieth century.

LOST HUDSON: 1950s–1970s

A stagnant economy led to architectural neglect in twentieth-century Hudson. The city's elegant middle-class houses were allowed to decay or were destroyed by fire, and the great houses of the comfortable merchants became apartment buildings or were demolished because they were simply too large to be affordably maintained. America had yet to see the growth of the architectural preservation movement and thus suffered irreparable loss to its architectural heritage.

Depredation was caused not only by neglect and the passage of time, but by planned demolition and ill-considered destruction. Hudson suffered, and occasionally suffers still, because of the often-unquestioned presumption that the old ought inevitably to make way for the new. What was viewed benignly, if misguidedly, as "urban renewal" ripped through town centers and erased their historic fabrics. These were the years when Penn Station in New York City was destroyed. Hudson, also, was touched by the dubious "progress" of urban renewal. Many historic houses were demolished to make way for "improvements."

Early photos of the city show some of the buildings that once stood where there are now empty parking lots or grim, featureless, 1960s-era structures. To make way for one such structure, the entire block between First and Front Street was obliterated. The 1837 Greek Revival Worth Hotel was razed. After having spent its declining years ignominiously converted into a garage, the incomparable Federal mansion built in the late eighteenth century by Captain John Hathaway was pulled down and replaced by the present one-story, cinder block warehouse. The entire area below Promenade Hill, which included some of Hudson's earliest houses, was demolished, as were large sections of Columbia and State streets. All were replaced with bland contemporary structures.

Fortunately, one brazen act of mass vandalism was thwarted. Some of Hudson's urban developers schemed to demolish the entire 400 block of Warren Street and Union Street in order to

Seventh Street Park with its fountain (now gone). To right and rear of the fountain is the Federal house that had formerly stood on the corner of Columbia and Seventh Street.

erect a supermarket and shopping plaza. But some of Hudson's longtime property owners who were attuned to the city's history and the value of its architecture refused to sell their homes. The scheme failed and the 400 block was saved.

Individual acts of neglect or misguided renovation also took their toll. Some churches lopped off their elegant steeples when it was bruited about that they might collapse if struck by lightning. The old orphan asylum was allowed to decay (and recently its great early trees were cut down). The park at Seventh Street was denuded of its elegant fountain. The Promenade's few remaining vestiges of nineteenth-century park architecture and furnishings disappeared, leaving St. Winifred to preside over a dreary, barren, unsafe, and uninviting expanse.

Many structures that escaped demolition or irreversible decay were altered or "modernized." Original clapboard was stripped away, ornamental cornices and decorations were removed, and early, small-paned windows were replaced. Sometimes entire eighteenth century or mid-nineteenth-century houses were boxed in beneath aluminum siding or perma-stone façades. Interiors suffered as well. High ceilings were dropped, knotty pine wallboard covered old plaster, moldings were removed, fireplace mantles were ripped out, parquet floors were covered with linoleum, and original fixtures were discarded as wreckers demolished history.

PORTRAIT GALLERY

Hudson Lost
1950s–2000

Hudson from the air, showing Front Street before the demolition of all of the buildings on the west side of the street. Collection of Jeremiah Rusconi.

Promenade Hill, Hudson, N.

The Promenade in the early twentieth century. Collection of Harry B. Halaco.

The Promenade in the 1950s.

Warren Street at Front Street in the nineteenth century. The block on the right above Front was demolished.

Intersection of Warren and Front streets circa 2005. Photograph by Sedat Pakay.

The south side of Warren Street below First Street in the 1860s. The entire block was demolished.

The same view today. Photograph by Sedat Pakay.

The Captain John Hathaway House, sometimes called the Beekman House. This building was demolished.

The site of the Hathaway/Beekman House today. Photograph by Sedat Pakay.

Historic Hudson ❋ **An Architectural Portrait**

*The corner of
North Fifth and
Warren Street in the
nineteenth century.
Now a parking lot.*

The Central Hotel was on the corner of South Fifth and Warren Street.

Hoysradt Hose above Fifth on Warren Street in the nineteenth century.

Italianate villa on Prospect Street in the 1860s. This building was demolished in the twentieth century. The path on the right is now Rossman Avenue. The garden below is now a Columbia Memorial Hospital parking lot.

Christ Church in the nineteenth century with its steeple.

The Hudson Asylum as the home of George Power. Collection of Harry B. Halaco.

The Hudson Library in the 1970s.

Willard Place in the 1890s.

Willard Place today. Photograph by Sedat Pakay.

Historic Hudson ❋ An Architectural Portrait

The house of artist Sanford Robinson Gifford stood on Sixth Street at the corner of Columbia Street. It was demolished in the mid-twentieth century and replaced with a parking lot.

*House formerly
on the corner of
Columbia and
Seventh Street.*

Federal house on the corner of Third and Union Street. Now a parking lot.

Historic Hudson ⊛ An Architectural Portrait

Federal house on the corner of Union and Second Street as it was in the nineteenth century.

The corner of Columbia and Fourth Street in the nineteenth century.

Second Empire building next to the St. Charles Hotel, before demolition. Now a parking lot.

Early house formerly on Warren at the end of Eighth Street in the nineteenth century.

Seventh Street Park in the early twentieth century.

The elegant Gifford Foundry on State Street.

Fountain, Public Square Park,
Hudson, N. Y.

The fountain in the park in the early twentieth century. Collection of Harry B. Halaco.

The fountain in 2005. Photograph by Sedat Pakay.

Hudson's alleys are original to the city's grid design.

A town pump on North Fifth Street.

EPILOGUE

HUDSON'S REVIVAL, 1980–2000

Fortunately, much of the past is recoverable. Those with a keen eye may walk down Hudson's streets and see beneath the failed taste and architectural brutalization of the 1950s, 1960s, and 1970s—behind the permastone and aluminum siding, the dropped ceilings and the plastic tile, the false, knotty pine paneling— honest and original houses waiting to be liberated. And liberation did come. Unlike many American small towns, which are still suffering the effects of America's hurried rejection of its past— marked by commercial consolidation (the flight to the malls) and by urban renewal—Hudson has had what might be called a lucky break. Into the social and economic vacuum that main street Hudson had become there came—slowly at first and then in larger numbers—individuals and groups of people who began to rent or to buy the empty shops and buildings on Warren Street. Shop after shop opened as more people came to take advantage of low rents and low real estate prices. Many of the newcomers bought residential properties as well. One by one, over a ten-year period from the early 1980s to the early 1990s, buildings were sold and new stores opened. Slowly, an empty Warren Street became a street full of busy stores again.

Hudson underwent a dramatic transformation from a depressed and despairing town with empty stores, empty streets, a failed economy, and faded but elegant houses, to becoming a thriving destination once again. Today, barely twenty years after the first antiques shop—the business that began this latest reversal of Hudson's fortunes—opened its doors, Hudson has about seventy antiques shops, a half-dozen upscale restaurants, several art galleries and bookstores, designer clothing and home furnishing stores, and the promise of more new stores opening soon. Complementing the expanding retail mix, the city now boasts four performance spaces that offer entertainment ranging from cabaret to avant-garde theater.

The news of Hudson's success has been the subject of extensive coverage in the national media. Its antiques shops are regularly mentioned in interior design magazines, and the city's attractions have found their way into the tourism pages of national publications. In consequence of its newfound popularity and prosperity, Hudson is experiencing a dizzying real estate boom.

While its streets are visited on weekends by out-of-town shoppers, there is also a more permanent effect in the form of a migration of people who have come to Hudson to make a new home. As the influx of homebuyers increased in the 1990s, some of Hudson's old-time residents soon began referring to the new residents of Hudson as the "New Proprietors," and there are some parallels. Like the merchant proprietors who came to Hudson two centuries earlier, these new arrivals saw potential waiting to be realized. And again like the old Proprietors, many of the newcomers were economic exiles seeking a place to make a new start. Some of the earliest of the "New Proprietors" were urban merchants tired of the skyrocketing prices of retail space in larger cities. Others were young singles, newly married couples, and older or retired people who found Hudson's real estate—low in price but large in space—more attractive than small and expensive big-city apartments.

Revival: the Robert and Seth Jenkins houses in 2005. Photograph by Will Bell.

Historic Hudson ❋ An Architectural Portrait

Among the earliest of these pioneers—and it did take a certain pioneering spirit to open a shop in a town largely devoid of business or to renovate a derelict house on a possibly dangerous street—was a large gay contingent. These were mostly gay men, often male couples, but there were some lesbian couples as well. They joined the small, but long-established, gay community that already existed in the city. Historically, gay people have often been in the forefront of urban neighborhood rehabilitation by opening shops, starting businesses, and renovating houses. "Old" Hudson sometimes feared this gay presence, but the fact was that Hudson's new gay inhabitants were far outnumbered by the new inhabitants who were not gay but who had come to Hudson for the same reasons—inexpensive housing and an inviting, if still gritty, small-town environment. Unlike some larger urban areas where gay people and non-gay people sometimes find themselves occupying seemingly demarcated and separate turf, in Hudson there is no gay "ghetto." Gay and non-gay communities mingle without friction and work together for the common good of the city they all treasure

Hudson has been reborn yet again, but this rebirth is not without its pangs. Suspicion of change and distrust of new residents who don't quite fit the small-town mold or adhere to its usually conservative standards is, of course, not unique to Hudson. This is a classic story—the old, familiar struggle between "us" and "them," between town and gown, between insiders and outsiders, between old and new. It is a story that is, in fact, as American as the dreams upon which the nation was founded. The history of Hudson is representative of the frictions and tensions, the problems, and the hope and promise that shaped both the past and the present of small-town life everywhere in America.

When it became clear some years ago, for example, that Hudson's Warren Street was fast becoming the nearly exclusive commercial purlieu of antique dealers, some native Hudsonians looked askance at the pricey merchandise, the newly painted and spruced-up shops, and the people the dealers attracted to the town, and they began to resent the vendors. Some understandably felt displaced by the new economy. An occasional letter to the local press expressed the wish that the dealers "go back where they came from." Most long-time residents took the changes in stride or welcomed the sudden rise in Hudson's fortunes, but among a vocal few, resentment against the dealers became a dislike of all the newcomers.

This tension became especially apparent in city politics when some new residents, more politically active than many of the older residents, began to attend the meetings of the city's Common Council. For many years Hudson's political affairs tended to be deliberated within the inner circles of whichever party was in power, and members of the Common Council were elected without challenge year after year. The public deliberations of the council were largely ignored by Hudson's citizens. Often the city's business was conducted and laws were passed before empty seats in the council chamber.

With the arrival of the new residents, a new political activism appeared on the scene. The usually empty chambers suddenly became filled with citizens asking questions about policy, mounting challenges to the decisions of the council, and engaging in often heated confrontations with the establishment.

Political activism in the city led also to social, preservationist, and environmental activism. In the early 1980s a group that included both locals and newcomers formed SHOW (Save Hudson's Only Waterfront) to protest and prevent the siting of an oil refinery on the city's riverfront. Though the plan was supported by the city government, the determination of SHOW members led to the project's defeat. This was the beginning of a new spirit of environmental activism in the city. A few years later, when the city announced that it would support the plans of a company that wished to build a large factory to manufacture dry-cleaning fluid on the waterfront, city residents, fearing the danger of pollution and hazards to the public health from the toxic liquid, once again rallied in protest and were so effective that the plant withdrew its application.

That spirit was soon called to an even greater task. When the announcement was made that a Swiss-owned company intended to build the nation's largest cement plant on an 1,800-acre site on a hill above Hudson and on several acres on its waterfront—a project again supported by the city establishment—a handful of veterans of the battle against the dry-cleaning fluid factory rallied together. They opposed the plant because of its vast size, the environmental dangers it posed, and its threat to the commercial and residential renaissance that was occurring in the city. Recalling stark images from the past of a riverfront degraded by industry and of a city that had sunk into decay when those industries failed, the citizens' group determined to defend Hudson's future.

It looked to be a lopsided contest. The citizens' group was rich in determination, but armed with only a modest war chest of donations. The cement company brought huge financial resources to the battle, plus a formidable legal team.

Calling itself the Friends of Hudson, the small grassroots citizens' organization grew steadily year by year, eventually extending beyond the city into a Hudson Valley-wide coalition. For nearly seven years the group worked to educate the public about the nature of the threat the plant presented, and initiated and pursued the complex and painstaking legal process needed to defeat the cement company's applications for permits to operate. Against all odds, the coalition was successful. Its permits denied by the state, the plant project was defeated and the cement company withdrew from the field. The coalition can now claim a permanent presence in Hudson, and within it old and new residents work in common cause for the good of the city.

There is also increased public concern for the preservation of the city's architectural heritage. In the years since the mid-1980s, Hudson's historic architecture has faced not only renewal and revitalization, but continued threat. The Hudson city administration has recently demolished some historically and architecturally important buildings. Familiar landmarks have met death by bulldozer—sometimes suddenly and without warning, as was the case with the important Romanesque Fourth Street School at the corner of Fourth and State Street, designed by Hudson architect Henry Moul.

Most recently, when it appeared that the irreplaceable 1818 almshouse that houses the Hudson Area Association Library faced an uncertain future that some feared might even mean demolition, it was public pressure from both old and new Hudsonians that forced the city and the school board (which owns the building) to make a meaningful gesture toward its preservation. The library board has taken the principled and courageous stand that it intends to keep the library there and will undertake a vigorous campaign to raise the money the structure so desperately needs.

This remarkable building—one of Hudson's earliest extant structures, at various times an almshouse, an asylum for the insane, an orphanage, and now a library—has nurtured, in a multitude of ways, many of Hudson's residents for almost two centuries, and if Hudson's residents are successful in finding the funds to restore it, it will continue to do so for generations yet to come.

Historic preservation has become an issue that has united the old and new residents, many of whom are members of Historic Hudson, the city's volunteer preservation group dedicated to preserving Hudson's historic buildings. As a consequence, the city government has also begun to move, if hesitantly, toward developing historic districts to protect the city's heritage. A Historic Preservation Commission has been created to designate landmarks and ensure their protection.

And so, while battles over turf, principles, and values still continue, there are signs that a growing sense of community may help to break down old barriers. As time has passed there has been some amelioration of the old suspicions. "Local" residents go to the trendy downtown restaurants and bars, drop in at gallery openings, and attend events at the local performance spaces. New residents have translated simple opposition into positive political action, and the extent of public support for change is evidenced by the fact that several new residents have taken seats on the Common Council.

Revival: the Seth Jenkins House in 2005. Photograph by Sedat Pakay.

And everywhere one looks, yet another Hudson house is born again. Houses hidden beneath aluminum siding have reappeared with original clapboard and six-over-six window sashes. Layers of paint have been removed, cornice moldings repaired, and formerly homely or nondescript houses have been revealed to be Federal gems or elegant Victorian survivals. Behind the façades, early interiors have been carefully restored. All around town the city's long-hidden architecture is being revealed again, more and more every day.

Up and down Warren Street and on every side street, this rebirth can be seen. Hudson's distinguished collection of buildings, grand and humble alike, charts the more than two centuries of Hudson's long journey. Each attests to the achievements of the women and men who participated in Hudson's history—every board and brick tells a story. The events of the past and those who lived in it are shadows at best, known to us from books and dusty public records, from hearsay and recollection.

But architecture is real. It is visible, and we can reach out and touch it. In all of Hudson's buildings, if we have the eyes to see them for what they are, the will to imagine what they were and yet could be, and the willingness to preserve and protect them as we must, we can locate both the dreams and the reality of the city's history. In a very real sense Hudson's buildings are its history, and like time machines they transport us to other days. Stand on any street and look around you: two centuries come alive before your eyes, past and present all in one.

Revival: Restored houses on lower Warren Street. Photograph by Sedat Pakay.

ABOUT THE AUTHOR

Byrne Fone is Emeritus Professor of English and American Literature at the City University of New York. He has written on eighteenth-century English and nineteenth-century American literature, and his work includes: *Masculine Landscapes, Walt Whitman and the Homoerotic Text; A Road to Stonewall: Homosexuality and Homophobia in English and American Literature; and The Columbia Anthology of Gay Literature,* which won the 1999 Lambda Literary Foundation Award. His most recent book is *Homophobia: A History,* published in hardcover by Metropolitan Books in 2000 and in paper by Picador in 2001. He has been active in Hudson community life for over twenty years, both in business and as a volunteer with many community organizations. He is a founding member of the Hudson Opera House and a member of Friends of Hudson. He has served on the boards of Time and Space Limited and the Hudson Opera House, and currently serves on the board of Historic Hudson. Byrne Fone lives in Hudson and France, and is finishing a novel.

NOTES

1. Elkanah Watson, *Men and Times of the Revolution, or the Memoirs of Elkanah Watson, Including His Journals of Travels in Europe and America, from the Year 1777 to 1842,* edited by Winslow C. Watson (New York, 1857). Quoted in Stephen B. Miller, *Sketches of Hudson* (Hudson, 1862), 103.

2. This and the following quotations from Henry Hudson's Journals quoted in Anna R. Bradbury, *History of the City of Hudson, N.Y.* (Hudson: Record Printing and Publishing Company, N.Y., 1908), xxvii–xxxi.

3. If indeed the Mohicans did have a village at the site of Hudson in 1609, they were destined not to remain there much longer. The later history of the Mohicans—the first inhabitants of Hudson and Columbia County—is a sad one. From a numerous tribe, masters of all the land now comprising Columbia, Rensselaer, and Berkshire counties, it was eventually reduced by war with the Iroquois Mohawks to a subject nation. Their tribe was diminished from thousands to a miserable few hundred. Their villages were destroyed and their ancient lands lost. Tradition says that the final struggle between the Mohawks and the Mohicans took place in 1628 not far from where Hudson now stands and it resulted in the defeat of the Mohicans, who fled across the Taghkanic Hills into Connecticut. Occasionally some Mohicans returned to their ancestral lands in Columbia County, but their fields and mountains now had been taken by others—the Dutch and the English. The Mohicans were no longer a nation. Reduced to penury, with no land of their own, and addicted to what they called "firewater," they had become vagabonds, and by the end of the seventeenth century the remnants of the tribe had indeed become the last of the Mohicans.

4. Margaret Schram, *Hudson's Merchants and Whalers: The Rise and Fall of a River Port, 1783–1850* (Hensonville, N.Y.: Black Dome Press, 2004), 9–11. Schram argues convincingly against the popular etymology of Claverack that derives the name from *Klover Reach,* i.e., from fields or reaches of clover that were said to have been everywhere.

5. Franklin Ellis, *History of Columbia County* (Philadelphia, 1878), 155. This and the following quoted material are from Ellis. I have drawn my remarks on Hudson's early history from Ellis, 152–165. Ellis's book takes the history of the city from the beginnings to 1878, and is the definitive nineteenth-century account. He draws upon both A. Gorham Worth (*Recollections of Hudson*) and Miller. Bradbury draws heavily upon Ellis, as does Margaret Schram, though Schram adds significantly to the store of information about early Hudson and is the definitive account of its whaling enterprise. I have adapted Worth, Miller, Bradbury, and Ellis in my summary of Hudson history, and just as I was finishing my work, I was able to see a proof of Schram and so added additional valuable materials that she provides.

6. Schram, op. cit., 29, 30.

7. Miller, op. cit., 51.

8. [Ignatius Jones], pseud. of A. Gorham Worth, *Recollections of Hudson,* (1847), 56. Worth's book is valuable because it gives an entertaining series of descriptions of Hudsonians alive in the eighteenth century.

9. Worth, op. cit., 24.

10. *See* Worth, 20–22; Miller, 85–88; Ellis, 181–18; and Schram, 153–157 on Hudson's Quakers.

11. *See* Ellis, 184–190; and Bradbury, 118–128 on Hudson's churches.

12. Quoted in Schram, 46.

13. Ellis, 157.

14. The preceding material on criminal activity was adapted from Bradbury, 42; and Miller, 25–26, both of whom quote from the minutes of the Hudson Common Council.

15. Bruce Hall, *Diamond Street: The Story of the Little Town with the Big Red Light District* (Hensonville, N.Y.: Black Dome Press, 1994), 17–20.

16. Quoted in Miller, 45–46.

17. Ellis, 190.

18. *See* Ellis, 190–196, and Bradbury, 126–135 on schools.

19. Quoted in Schram, 74–75.

20. *See* Miller, 46–52 on military and marching bands.

21. Bradbury, 188.

22. Ibid., 79.

23. *See* Ellis, 161–162.

24. Schram, 105.

25. Ibid., 97.

26. Quoted in Miller, 104.

27. *See* Ruth Piwonka and Roderic H. Blackburn, *A Visible Heritage: Columbia County, New York, a History in Art and Architecture* (Hensonville, N.Y.: Black Dome Press, 1996), 19, for a full account of the county's architectural styles.

28. Miller, 101.

29. Advertisement for the Flag House, reproduced in Robert Terry, *The Hudsonian: Old Times and New* (Hudson: Edwin Rowley printer, 1895) and in Schram, 48.

30. Miller, 14.

31. Ellis, 64.

32. Schram, 146.

33. Ibid., 58.

34. Ellis, 165.

35. Worth, 4-5.

36. Miller, 106.

37. Bradbury, 188.

38. Ibid., 122.

39. Ibid., 214.

INDEX

Page numbers in italics refer to captions for illustrations.

Historic Hudson

The pictures in this book come primarily from the Historic Hudson/Rowles Studio Collection of Historic Photographs of the city of Hudson. This collection numbers nearly 300 images dating from the mid-nineteenth to the early twentieth century. The earlier images in the collection, all glass negatives, were taken by Frank Forshew, who was born in Hudson in 1827. Forshew was a pioneer in the early days of photography and became known in the area and nationally as a portrait photographer. In 1865 he erected the brick block in Hudson that bears his name and where, at what is now 441 Warren Street, he had his studio. The later images in the collection, glass and gelatin negatives, were taken by Forshew's successor, Samuel Rowles, whose Rowles Studio gives the collection its name. It was from the successor to Rowles that Historic Hudson acquired the present collection of glass negatives, many of which are reproduced here.

When Rowles Studio closed and the building was purchased in the 1980s by local resident and interior designer David Whitcomb, many broken glass negatives in irreparable condition were discovered. From these and from the scope of the intact collection, it seems quite possible that Forshew and Rowles photographed most of the streets and a large number of the buildings in the city of Hudson. It is tantalizing to speculate that at one time a complete photographic record of Hudson's buildings may have existed.

While the present collection has gaps in the imagery, many of Forshew's images were reproduced in the early part of the twentieth century as postcards, and a large number of these, collected by a Hudson resident, the late Herman Roth, and later acquired by local resident Harry B. Halaco, have been used in this book to supplement the original images so as to give as complete a record of the city as possible. Further images not in the collection, but most probably taken by Forshew or Rowles, have been obtained from the extensive collection of Hudson images owned by Debbie and the late Hank DiCintio, and from photographs in the collection of Jeremiah Rusconi. The author invites anyone who finds errors in attribution to contact him.

Historic Hudson is compiling as complete an image collection as possible of Hudson's buildings and invites anyone who possesses images of the city and wishes to share them to contact Historic Hudson or the author. To assist those who own or have purchased one of Hudson's buildings and wish to restore the structure with historic accuracy, Historic Hudson will provide individual owners with a copy of the image of the building or buildings in question free of charge if the building is in its image collection.

Historic Hudson is a not-for-profit corporation founded in 1996 to promote the preservation of the unique architectural heritage of the city of Hudson, New York. Hudson is considered by many to be a veritable dictionary of American architectural style, comprising a remarkable collection of largely intact eighteenth, nineteenth, and early-twentieth-century buildings.

It is the mission of Historic Hudson to preserve that heritage, a mission that is achieved through advocacy and public events and programs that disseminate information about the city's history and foster appreciation for its historic architecture. Among its programs are the annual Preservation Awards, lectures and exhibits on various aspects of Hudson's architecture and history, the creation of walking tour guides of the city that describe street by street and by date and style Hudson's many historic buildings, and the maintenance and publication of the Historic Hudson/Rowles Studio Collection of glass negative photographs, numbering nearly 300 rare images of the city of Hudson from the nineteenth and early twentieth century.

When the situation demands, the organization ensures the survival of buildings through acquisition, stabilization, and resale to new owners committed to restoration and preservation, a process that in 2001 saved from demolition an eighteenth-century frame house at 126 Warren Street.

Historic Hudson is also the advocate for and steward of the 1812 Plumb–Bronson House, which was designated a National Historic Landmark in 2003. Originally a house of Federal design built for Samuel Plumb, who followed the original Proprietors to Hudson from New England, the house was "refitted" in 1839 in the Picturesque style by the leading architect of the day, Alexander Jackson Davis, who was commissioned by a later owner, Dr Oliver Bronson. The Plumb–Bronson House is located on the grounds of the Hudson Correctional Facility. In concert with that facility and the New York State Department of Corrections, Historic Hudson has acquired a long-term lease, which will make Historic Hudson legal steward of the Plumb–Bronson House and allow the organization to move forward to stabilize and preserve this remarkable structure.

For more information about Historic Hudson, please visit our website at www.historichudson.org. Basic membership in Historic Hudson is $25 for individuals, $40 for couples or families. To join Historic Hudson, please telephone 518 828-1785 or write to: Historic Hudson, PO Box 804, Hudson, New York 12534.